Praise for *Choose Compassion*

'This book is a gem. It is full of up-to-date findings, reflections on crucial conceptual issues and self-help guidance all presented in an easy-to-understand way. It will be essential reading for anyone interested in how to cultivate and promote caring and compassionate behaviours in oneself and many areas of life.' – Professor Paul Gilbert OBE, author of *The Compassionate Mind*

'If you want to understand compassion you need look no further than this book. James Kirby seamlessly and compellingly weaves together current events, ethical dilemmas and therapeutic practice. *Choose Compassion* is moving, informative and highly engaging: an essential and stimulating guide to the value/quality we all so badly need at this troubled time.' – Jennifer Nadel, co-director of Compassion in Politics, and co-author of *We: A manifesto for women everywhere*

'*Choose Compassion* made me want to be a better person – and, more importantly, gave me hope that was something within my reach. Hopeful, friendly, accessible – it's like listening to a smart friend explaining those psychological and ethical concepts you've always wondered about.' – Tegan Taylor, health and science reporter, ABC

'*Choose Compassion* is truly a tour de force, combining everyday examples of compassion mixed with hard science to make a compelling case that one should choose compassion as the ethos of one's life.' – James R Doty MD, founder and director of the Stanford University Center for Compassion and Altruism Research and Education (CCARE), and author of *Into the Magic Shop: A neurosurgeon's quest to discover the mysteries of the brain and the secrets of the heart*

T0246665

'A compassionate response to stress and pain is at the heart of human life, and James Kirby brings us a masterful, practical guide to it. Grounded in fascinating research, his writing is friendly, deeply touching, and always useful. While compassion is natural, sometimes we block it due to thoughts about ourselves or others. Dr Kirby shows us how to find the inner freedom in a compassion that nurtures oneself while having goodwill toward others, even in challenging relationships. Charming and engaging, each page shines with the kindness and genuine brilliance of its author. A gem.' – Rick Hanson PhD, author of *Buddha's Brain: The practical neuroscience of happiness, love, and wisdom*

'To anyone despairing at the state of the world right now, grab this book. It is a handbook for humanity, a deep re-affirmation of our innate compassion for others and the urgency to reclaim it, everywhere and anywhere we can, today.' – Kon Karapanagiotidis OAM, Founder and CEO of the Asylum Seeker Resource Centre

'Powerful, fun, and insightful. This book makes you think creatively about compassion and gives us hope that we can each do something to help each other.' – Scott Barry Kaufman PhD, author of *Transcend* and *Choose Growth*, and host of *The Psychology Podcast*

James Kirby is the co-director of the Compassionate Mind Research Group at the University of Queensland. He studies the effectiveness of Compassion Focused Therapy interventions in helping with the self-criticism and shame that underpin many depression and anxiety disorders. James also works as a clinical psychologist in private practice. This is his first book.

JAMES
KIRBY

Choose
Compassion

Why it matters
and how it works

UQP

First published 2022 by University of Queensland Press
PO Box 6042, St Lucia, Queensland 4067 Australia

University of Queensland Press (UQP) acknowledges the Traditional Owners and their custodianship of the lands on which UQP operates. We pay our respects to their Ancestors and their descendants, who continue cultural and spiritual connections to Country. We recognise their valuable contributions to Australian and global society.

uqp.com.au
reception@uqp.com.au

Copyright © James Kirby 2022
The moral rights of the author have been asserted.

This book is copyright. Except for private study, research, criticism or reviews, as permitted under the Copyright Act, no part of this book may be reproduced, stored in a retrieval system, or transmitted in any form or by any means without prior written permission. Enquiries should be made to the publisher.

Cover design by Christabella Designs
Cover photograph by art_of_sun/Shutterstock
Author photograph by Jonathan Brazil
Typeset in 12.5/17.5 pt Bembo Std by Post Pre-press Group, Brisbane
Printed in Australia by McPherson's Printing Group

 **Queensland Government** University of Queensland Press is supported by the Queensland Government through Arts Queensland.

  University of Queensland Press is assisted by the Australian Government through the Australia Council, its arts funding and advisory body.

A catalogue record for this book is available from the National Library of Australia.

ISBN 978 0 7022 6564 8 (pbk)
ISBN 978 0 7022 6709 3 (epdf)
ISBN 978 0 7022 6710 9 (epub)

University of Queensland Press uses papers that are natural, renewable and recyclable products made from wood grown in well-managed forests and other controlled sources. The logging and manufacturing processes conform to the environmental regulations of the country of origin.

For my family

Contents

Prologue

You are out doing your morning exercise. While walking, you notice a child has fallen into a small pond. They are struggling. It looks like they are drowning. What do you do?

For many this is a no-brainer: you help. It would be hard – almost impossible – to imagine a scenario in which you do not help, despite the fact you would get wet, it would delay your exercise and it would be somewhat inconvenient. Still, by incurring these low-level costs you would be saving a child's life.

Many reading this book will be familiar with this thought experiment, referred to as 'the drowning child'. Peter Singer created it to put to students taking his ethics course every year. He adds a further seemingly simple but important moral question to his students: 'Are we obligated to help the child?', to which the students almost always respond, 'Absolutely.'

At this point in the experiment we could imagine varying possibilities that shift the degree of uncertainty. Perhaps there are other people around the pond who might be able to assist, or maybe you aren't 100% sure that your efforts will make a difference. Do you still decide to help? Or you might need to leave your phone on the bank of the pond and there is a good chance it will get stolen. Do you still decide to help? What if you saved a child from the pond only last week?

The final twist: imagine if the child was in a distant country, but in a similar situation, and it was equally within your means to save them. Do you still decide to help?

How do we – how do you – make the decision to act compassionately towards others who are suffering? How do we weigh up the costs (e.g., wet clothes) and benefits (e.g., a child's life)?

We have experienced a massive disruption to our everyday lives during the COVID-19 pandemic. Many of us have incurred costs on a daily basis in order to protect others. These costs are, admittedly, relatively low: for example, wearing masks, keeping socially distanced, getting vaccinated, limiting our travel, staying home if sick and washing our hands. But how long are we willing to put up with these costs? For many of us, there comes a point when we start to feel like we can't continue, when we want to return to 'normal'.

While balancing the stress of the pandemic, we've also been flooded with political ideology and discourse, with some politicians exploiting the situation to maximise their chance of getting votes. It can be difficult to process conflicting information about the right way to act in a sea of tragedy. Who do we decide to trust?

On the surface it might seem that making decisions to act compassionately when confronted with suffering is easy. You just do it. But real life is messy. The way our brains are designed, and the emotions we feel, can get in the way.

Let's have a look at another famous thought experiment, 'the trolley problem'. In this scenario five people are tied to railway tracks and a train is coming towards them. You are in a position where you can alter the train's trajectory to a new track by pulling a lever. This will save those five lives. However, on this new track there is one person tied up, which the train will kill. You have two options: do nothing or pull the lever. What do you decide? If you pull the lever fewer people die, but you will have actively participated, albeit in a small way, in the death of one person.

Overwhelmingly people say they would pull the lever. It seems like the morally right thing to do, possibly even the more compassionate thing to do. I'd propose there is one version in which it is almost guaranteed people won't pull the lever, and that is if the single person tied to the tracks is their child. Rightly or wrongly, parents value the life of their child more than the lives of five strangers.

There are many variations of this thought experiment, and there are also critics of it. The point of bringing it up here though is to show how we have in-built biases that make us value some lives more than others. This makes compassion complicated. If a person values their child's life over those of five strangers, can they still be called a compassionate person? If you were ruled only by logic, you might still pull the lever. But we all have emotions and feelings that we can't avoid.

When confronted with decisions, even if they are hypothetical, we can experience a level of mental fatigue. Every day we have to make choices: what to wear, what to eat, what to read and, critically, what to watch on Netflix. Humans find making decisions hard. It requires mental effort.[1] Some of us get overwhelmed by restaurant menus, and generally we find it easier to make a decision from three options than three thousand options. At an extreme, though, *Sophie's Choice*, in which a mother has to choose which of her two children will be killed, shows us how difficult decision-making is when suffering is involved.

Human beings aren't perfect. We can be irrational, biased, sexist, prejudiced and more. But we can also be profoundly compassionate. Over the course of this book I am going to examine not only what compassion is, but also how we go about deciding to be compassionate. I will look at how our emotions can get the better of us, and how our logic can at times make us appear cold-hearted. I will consider humankind's confusing contradictions, such as ignoring mass levels of suffering but then going to extraordinary lengths to prevent the pain of just one person. I will look at how compassion is developed within our families and cultures, and how compassion can be healing for those experiencing mental-health difficulties. By going on this journey I hope to answer a big question: with climate change, mass extinction, genocide and war, can humans really lay claim to being compassionate?

I think we can.

1

What is compassion?

When you think of compassion, what comes to mind? Kindness, understanding, tenderness, empathy, maybe warmth? Compassion can be all those things – but it is much more. And at its heart is courage and wisdom, two things that people rarely mention when they talk about compassion.

I start almost every workshop, lecture or therapy session I give on compassion asking what the word brings to mind. I then ask, 'If I were to see you being compassionate, what would I see?' Common responses include listening, being present, touching or giving a hug. These capture some of what I mean by courage and wisdom. But to fully unpack it, I pose a third and final question: 'How would you like someone to be compassionate towards you?' At this point someone usually says, 'I'd like some space.' Other common responses include wanting to be heard, to be given time, to be validated and to be touched. As you will have noticed, there can be overlaps in how we give and receive compassion, but there are also slight differences.

The essential feature of compassion that is always missed when going through this series of questions is *suffering*. Compassion is only compassion when there is suffering. And compassion is motivated by alleviating that suffering. In the scientific community, compassion is defined as 'a sensitivity to suffering in self and others, with a commitment to try to alleviate and prevent it'.[1] This is not quite the same as kindness, empathy, sympathy or altruism. When suffering is at the heart of the matter, the two qualities that are most important are courage and wisdom.

But how do courage and wisdom connect to compassion? We can better understand this by considering the nurses and doctors who placed themselves at enormous risk in the early stages of the pandemic. I remember speaking to my brother, a respiratory physiotherapist who was working on the COVID-19 intensive care ward at the Royal London Hospital at the time. I asked him whether he had to be on the intensive care ward, and he told me he did. He had been trained to help people with their breathing, so that was where he had to be. This is heroic compassion. It takes enormous courage to put your life at risk to protect others from suffering.

But my brother wasn't just running into the ward wanting to help. He was taking the necessary precautions, like all healthcare staff, by wearing personal protective equipment. Wearing this gear was highly uncomfortable, and even painful, but endured daily because it enabled workers to help those suffering without exposing themselves to higher levels of risk. That is wise.

Tragically, people were dying alone in intensive care units with family unable to be with them due to the nature of the virus. So what did healthcare workers do? They stayed and held the hands of those dying patients, knowing that being with someone in those final moments is better than being alone. That is wise and courageous compassion.

For many, compassion is equated with gentle and comforting actions. But this is just one example of compassionate behaviour, and there are thousands of possibilities. The compassionate action that is taken depends on a number of factors, including your skills. While I may wish that I had the skills to develop a vaccine, for example, I don't. There are other important things that I can do though that will help prevent infection during a pandemic, such as wearing a mask. In some ways the pandemic unleashed our compassion – our want and need to be helpful to others – on a grand scale.

Compassion is powerful because rather than running away from suffering, it turns towards it. I work as a clinical psychologist, and the one thing in therapy I am in constant awe of is the courage my patients have in walking through the therapy door. People typically go to see a psychologist about something that they are scared of, dislike or find hard. When they see a psychologist they have courageously chosen to talk about and work on the thing that distresses them for 50 minutes.

When we don't know how to help ourselves or others who are suffering, the wisest thing we can do is seek help, whether it be from nurses, doctors, psychologists, social workers, midwives, physiotherapists, teachers or scientists. For example, if you were drowning in the Brisbane River and I saw you, I might think, 'I have to jump in and save you.' But if in midair I remembered that I can't swim, all of a sudden two people would need to be rescued. More helpful actions would include calling out for help or ringing emergency services.

Knowing what you are able to do and then *actually doing it* is the important thing, whether it's a big action or small. It is no good just thinking about it. Hence why many of us get angry when we hear 'thoughts and prayers' as a response to preventable disasters.

Let's take the case of Brian. Brian has recently experienced a loss; his father who he was close to has died. How might Brian be feeling? Here we can use our empathy, which is often regarded as the process of feeling and thinking like another person.[2] So Brian might be feeling sad, and he might be wishing his father was still alive. Empathy helps us know this information, but it doesn't tell us how to use it.

Our automatic response to hearing Brian's news might be sympathy. This is when we are emotionally moved by the stories or news we hear or read about. However, sympathy doesn't tell us what to do either.

We can be kind to Brian. But what action would kindness take in this situation? At its core, kindness is about treating others as kin or taking action to benefit them. Kindness is linked to happiness and wellbeing, so a kind act for Brian might be to take him to a movie to get his mind off things or offer to do something practical to help him out: cook dinner, mow the lawn.

But do these kind acts address his suffering – his sadness over the loss of his father? They might, but only a little bit. Still, a kind act might open the door for Brian to speak to us about things that are troubling him. Thus, kindness can be a gateway to compassion, but is not compassion itself.

There is a lot of overlap between kindness and compassion, but at its core compassion focuses on suffering, while kindness focuses on wellbeing or happiness. One could argue that a kind act is to a degree compassionate, but you couldn't say all kind acts are compassionate. Some kind gestures, like buying a present or phoning a friend to say hello, don't include suffering at all. Kindness is often about what we *want*, and compassion about what we *need*. The cleanest way to differentiate acts of kindness and compassion is by context. If the context is one of suffering then the act is best considered compassionate. For example, the act of listening to a friend who recently attended a wedding would be kind, as you have provided them the opportunity to talk about something joyous. But change this to listening to a friend who recently attended a funeral, then it is compassionate. The act is the same, listening, but the context of a funeral involves suffering and thus makes the act compassionate.

Kindness is very important from an evolutionary perspective at forming coalitions and helping with cooperation.[3] For example, if you do something kind for someone it will often be reciprocated later. This is sometimes referred to as 'reciprocal altruism', which is when we act in a way that might be costly to us but helps another, knowing that it will be repaid later. We often engage in reciprocal altruism with our neighbours, and countries we share borders with, as we are physically close to each other and it makes life easier for the both of us. Many birds and mammals do this, such as when grooming each other.

Kind acts signal to others that they are important to us. Doing a deliberately kind act for someone else means you have thought about that other person positively when they are not around. This is crucially important in building friendships and trust networks. To be held positively in other people's minds when we are not around can help us feel like we matter, that people care about us, that we are safe. Many of us worry a great deal about what others think of us and what is said about us when we are not around. Kind acts are a way of mitigating that worry and forming strong bonds.

So what would a compassionate response to Brian look like? Here we channel our attention to his suffering: his grief. That might mean a compassionate response would address Brian's loss. He could be angry about his father's death. We could visit Brian, ask him directly about how he is feeling and make time to listen. Physical proximity might also allow us to offer more than words, like a hug. All these are efforts to connect with Brian, knowing that losing someone can create a sense of aloneness.

Presence and touch are incredibly powerful at connecting people. In moments of loss we also tend to realise how limited words can be. Nurses often state that the best way to be compassionate to patients is to hold their hands. One study found the distress experienced when having an fMRI is reduced significantly by holding the hand of a loved one.[4]

A patient of mine experienced the profound impact touch can have. She had to go to hospital for a fairly routine procedure, but she is terrified of needles. To make matters worse, the procedure was to rule out cancer. All the doctors were extremely positive, indicating that they were simply confirming that there was no cancer present. Nevertheless, the slim chance it could be was causing some anxiety for my patient. When I saw her in therapy after the procedure, I asked her how it all went. She told me that when she was on the cold theatre bed, feeling quite alone and scared but trying not to show it, her doctor reached down and held her hand. He held it firmly, giving it a reassuring squeeze. She said there was a real feeling in the way he did it. She said, 'He was holding my hand compassionately.' No words were spoken between them. But my patient said it made all the difference.

It is these kinds of moments in health care that can have profound and lasting effects for patients.[5] Indeed, my patient said, 'I doubt my doctor thought anything of it, but I will never forget that compassionate touch.' Studies have looked at touch and found that, even if we cannot see the other person, we can detect the feeling they are trying to convey through their hand.[6]

When we talk about compassion, often all those qualities of empathy, sympathy and kindness are involved. But it can be helpful to recognise how these qualities are different, to better understand that compassion is not just another form of kindness. Its aim is to alleviate suffering, while kindness promotes happiness, empathy mirrors the feelings and thoughts of others, and sympathy is our automatic emotional reaction to situations.

When I'm running workshops on compassion one of the most common comments I receive is that empathy, not compassion, is the most important quality for helping others. But empathy has limitations and drawbacks, as Professor Paul Bloom outlines so well in his book *Against Empathy*.[7] At its core this is an issue of confusion between motivation and competency. Compassion is a motivation – the desire to alleviate suffering – while empathy is a competency, or a skill we have. The late psychoanalyst Heinz Kohut puts it simply: empathy can be used for different purposes. If you really want to hurt somebody, you use your empathic skills to get a sense of what might do the most damage.[8]

Empathy isn't particularly helpful for ethical and moral decision-making either. A classic experimental study by Professor Daniel Batson and colleagues is often shared to illustrate this point.[9] In the experiment, participants were told they would listen to an interview of a child with a terminal condition. Participants were told to either listen to the interview objectively or listen empathically. They then listened to the story of a ten-year-old girl named Sheri Summers who has a fatal disease. Sheri is on the waitlist for treatment that could prolong her life. Sadly she has weeks or months before that will happen. After hearing this, the participants were then asked whether they would fill out a special form to move Sheri up the waitlist. Around 75% of participants who were instructed to feel empathy filled out the form to move Sheri up the list. But, as Batson and his colleagues point out, this is a conflict of justice and morality. By doing this, other children above her on the waitlist, some of whom may be more deserving, will have to wait longer.

Another limitation of empathy is that it is easy to empathise with one person but not a large group. This is sometimes referred to as 'the identifiable victim effect'. This effect is why charities in their advertising often depict one child or one vulnerable person as opposed to hundreds, knowing the image of one can move us to donate our money or time to the cause. This was the case for Sheri Summers as well; the participants could identify with her, but they didn't know the other children.

When it comes to empathy we are often instructed to imagine ourselves in someone else's shoes. This can be problematic. Yes, I can try to imagine what it would be like to be Brian, losing his father, but I would be imagining that situation as me, not as Brian. And the way I experience the loss of my father will be different to how Brian experiences it. Bloom once referred to this as 'the arrogance of empathy'. For example, someone with a stable home could imagine being homeless, but if they have never experienced it firsthand would they really know what it feels like to be homeless every minute of every day? And, crucially, do they have to do that to be compassionate to the homeless?

This begs the question, do we need to be 'moved' to be compassionate? Being moved often connotes an emotional experience. If all compassionate acts require us to be moved, it will be difficult to make any significant impact on the amount of suffering in the world. In some ways this is also paradoxical. Sympathy is our automatic emotional reaction to someone else's state or condition.

People often say, 'I don't want your sympathy' when they still want to be helped. In response to this, I sometimes ask patients, 'Would you prefer me not to be emotionally moved by the news of your father passing away? How would it make you feel if I wasn't emotionally moved, if I wasn't sympathetic towards your distress?' This can lead to a response of, 'I would prefer if you were empathic.' But that means I need to try to imagine myself as you, feeling the pain and grief of the loss of your father. It's almost sadistic. The idea is, basically, I can't help you unless I feel the same emotion that you do. But patients who are experiencing a panic attack don't want their therapist to do the same. Instead the therapist should help, using the knowledge they've acquired through their training.

So sympathy and empathy can be very helpful informers to compassionate behaviours, but they aren't a requirement.

Compassion is also contextual: how we show compassion will depend on the type of suffering we encounter. If you were to see someone sad, your compassionate response might be to hug them, trying to convey a sense of gentleness with your body language. If you were to see someone angry, your compassionate response might be to validate their anger or ask them with an air of urgency, 'What's wrong?' If you were to see someone who seemed anxious, your compassionate response might be to encourage them or reassure them, trying to convey a sense of confidence and calm. If the suffering were more physical than emotional, your compassionate response might differ again. If you were to see someone in a car crash, your compassionate response might be to call emergency services. If you were to see someone in palliative care, your compassionate response might be more gentle and quiet.

In these examples the emotions and situations are different, yet they all include two key features: suffering and action to alleviate that suffering.

Every day we encounter moments of suffering, whether it be walking past a person who is homeless in the city, observing a colleague at work in emotional distress, or viewing victims of international conflict in the media. Despite all these types of suffering being different, one thing remains the same: we have to decide whether or not to act. But how do we make this choice? Australians believe we should be more compassionate and do more to help people facing tough times,[10] but how do we harness these intentions and transform them into everyday compassionate behaviours in our communities?

Sometimes our emotions can move us to do something, but our morals and ethics can be orthogonal to our feelings, complicating the decision-making process. When deciding to act compassionately our deliberation can sometimes lead to inaction. Phrases like 'I just don't have the time' and 'I am too busy right now' are familiar. Another powerful blocker to compassionate action is the person being different to us, as we find it easier to empathise with those similar to us.[11]

There are many studies that document how categorising people into groups can stop us from helping each other. One experiment involved the fans of two rival soccer teams.[12] Participants viewed a fan of the opposing team in pain, and were given the choice to help or not. Helping would mean enduring some of the physical pain themselves to reduce the other's pain. Not helping meant the rival would continue to experience the physical pain, and the participant would be given the option of watching another soccer video (so not seeing the pain) or continuing to watch that person in pain. When the fan in pain supported the same team as the participant (in-group condition), they helped them approximately 65% of the time. When it was a rival (out-group condition), that rate of helping dropped to 45%. And when the participant chose not to help, 25% chose to watch their rival in physical pain, but when it was the in-group only 8% watched.

As a way of demonstrating the effect of in-groups and out-groups I'd like you to consider a moment when you were compassionate to someone. Who was the target of your compassion? What did you do to show compassion? One thing that often stands out is that the target of our compassion is someone close to us, such as a family member or a friend. This could be because in-group members are people we see more of, and proximity is a key determinant to compassionate action. Indeed, it was at the heart of Peter Singer's drowning child thought experiment.

It is crucial to recognise the contextual factors that underpin our compassionate behaviours. The way compassion is expressed in individualistic Western cultures like Australia and the US might be quite different to more collectivist countries such as Japan. Equally, one could have a loving and trusting family environment where compassion is freely shown when needed, but a work culture that is competitive and ruthless in which compassion is seen as a weakness, and not shown at all.

Another key factor in compassionate behaviour is whether we even observe suffering in the first place. How much suffering does there need to be for you to notice? Does the person have to be at rock bottom for you to act? We refer to this as your 'sensitivity to suffering'. How loud does the suffering need to be for you to hear it? We all vary, with some of us more sensitive to some types of suffering than others. Many of us can be completely unaware of the intense suffering of people we love. Humans are very good at hiding suffering. Some people, though, are like Sherlock Holmes in their ability to pick up on small signals that something isn't quite right.

There are so many factors that affect our willingness to help others. One powerful blocker to compassionate behaviour is time. When rushed, people don't stop to help others. Professors John Darley and Daniel Batson did a seminal study on helpful behaviour, commonly referred to as 'the good Samaritan study'.[13] Each participant had to teach the good Samaritan parable to a university class, and on the way to that class they passed a stranger who needed help. This is of course the crux of the parable, in which a hapless victim on the side of the road is passed by a bunch of holy individuals – until a non-holy Samaritan takes the time to stop and help out. In the Darley and

Batson study, participants had to walk across campus to teach the class, and on the way they passed a confederate (someone in on the study) who needed help. Participants were in one of three categories: they had plenty of time to get to class, they were on time, or they were running late to the class. What they found was 63% of participants in the plenty-of-time condition stopped to help the stranger, 45% in the on-time condition stopped to help, and only 10% in the running-late condition helped.

It also depends whether we are emotionally moved by someone's suffering or whether we consider it in a more thoughtful or deliberate fashion. An example of the cognitive or deliberative pathway to compassion would be if you saw someone you didn't like suffering. You might not be emotionally moved by their suffering, but your moral principle to be compassionate when you can would lead you to help the person anyway.

A group called Effective Altruism[14] runs on this deliberative-pathway principle. The aim of the group is to determine what charities are effective, relying on a data-driven approach that combines artificial intelligence programming and algorithms to evaluate the lives saved by monetary donations. You can then choose to donate to those charities deemed effective, knowing this action will lead to greater outcomes. Or, if you would rather, you can donate to Effective Altruism Funds, where they take the guesswork out for you and their team distributes your donation to the causes you have selected as important (e.g., animal welfare, global health or development). The major principle behind the model is maximising utility, also called 'utilitarian ethics'. Your $50 donation to Effective Altruism Funds will help reduce more suffering than donating to another charity that you might personally like, but that doesn't have the same impact. People in the Effective Altruism community often give the example of people donating to guide dogs, which are popular, but not to malaria nets, which are able to save more lives for the same amount of money.[15] Effective Altruism tries to take the emotion out of donating, therefore removing the biases we have for certain groups.

It is also necessary to identify when action is more helpful than inaction. For example, when Hurricane Katrina devastated New Orleans in 2005, many people around the US wanted to do something immediately to help. This led to an outpouring of donations. To help those who had lost everything, people sent clothes, food, toys and more.[16] This meant that government resources that were desperately needed to help with evacuation efforts had to be redirected to process donations. People's attempts to be helpful were actually causing more problems. And despite calls to stop sending in donations, they kept coming.

Many of us can be so personally distressed when hearing devastating news that we feel compelled to do something. But this action can become more about alleviating our own personal distress than that of the people we are trying to help.[17] This is an example of unwise compassionate helping. Our capacity for distress tolerance is an important determinant of compassionate behaviour. Sometimes the best response in times of crises is to wait – easier said than done if we are being flooded with images of devastation, conflict and war.

When we extend compassion to others, we feel good, particularly if the action has been accepted and was helpful. However, if our compassionate behaviour has a negative impact on others or ourselves this might reduce the likelihood of us acting compassionately in the future. The movie *Frozen* has a good example of this: in the process of helping Anna, Kristoff's sled is destroyed, and so he decides to never help anyone again.

If our help is rejected we can be less likely to help again. But in these instances we have often made the situation more about ourselves than the person we are trying to help. It is important when acting compassionately that we don't take rejections personally. For example, if I call Brian to see how he is feeling about the loss of his father, he may respond to my enquiry with anger, saying he doesn't want to talk about it and I should know better than to ask. If my response to this is to call Brian an arsehole, I have made the situation about me and not about Brian, who is clearly suffering. The aim here is to see that Brian's anger is just him projecting his grief. He's not really angry with me, as the situation isn't about me; he's angry with the pain he is experiencing. This doesn't mean I give up. I might give it some time, talk to his partner and see how things are.

There is a feedback loop with compassionate behaviour, as we can refine and modify what we do based on how it is received.

Thankfully, studies have found that compassionate acts are contagious.[18] When we receive compassion from someone, we are more likely to be compassionate to someone else. We pay it forward. We don't even have to be recipients of an action to be infected by compassionate behaviour. Simply observing someone being compassionate increases the likelihood we will be compassionate to someone else.[19]

Compassion is not solely determined by the success of the outcome. You can be motivated to be compassionate, and the method of how you actualise that compassionate intent can be true and good, but the outcomes don't always go the way we would hope. That is not a failure. Unfortunately, many can be focused solely on the outcome. For some people, if they don't see their action resolving suffering then they believe it is not worth worrying or thinking about. They can get caught up with thoughts like 'There's nothing you can do, so just get over it'.

Compassion extends beyond dealing with something that is causing us physical pain. You can have a doctor who just cures your pain, or one who does the same thing but with warmth, being emotionally supportive. Both doctors have cured your pain, but only the latter is described as compassionate by patients.

Compassion also doesn't offer easy answers for the moral dilemmas that we face as a species. For example, humans have tested on animals for decades to understand illness and produce medical products to save lives. This is a moral dilemma. Many animals will endure long-lasting suffering and die for humans to benefit, but the resulting medical advancements extend our lives and in some cases save millions of people. But still, the welfare of animals matters.

During this pandemic some new possibilities have emerged for us to address suffering. For example, there is a movement called 'the human-challenge trials', in which volunteers help determine the effectiveness of new vaccines. Over 38,000 volunteers from 166 countries have signed up for human-challenge trials to help with COVID-19 vaccination testing. Once signed up the volunteers are randomised to receive the vaccine or a placebo. They are then exposed to the COVID-19 virus. For those with the placebo this is a big risk, but excellent medical care is available to help manage the symptoms.

Participants in these trials speed up the understanding of which vaccines are effective for humans and which aren't, making it possible to have the vaccine sooner to save lives. It is incredible we have volunteers willing to do this, and it takes away the need to test on animals. Given these are human problems, should we not at least see what humans are willing to do to save human lives?

As a final point, creativity is important when it comes to compassion. Some professions might be considered on the surface to be more compassionate than others, such as healthcare work, but we don't all have to go out and become healthcare workers to create more compassionate communities. Indeed, the philosophers Arthur Schopenhauer and Friedrich Nietzsche had serious debates over this. Schopenhauer was very big on the idea that compassion is the most noble pursuit and should be followed at all costs. Nietzsche was concerned about the harm this might do if we were to put compassion first and neglect our own passions. He gave the example of Beethoven, and how we wouldn't have his music if he had been pressured to pursue a more 'compassionate' career. But Beethoven has had a greater impact on humankind by pursuing his love of music than he would have had doing something else.

This is a really important point. There is no one compassionate action: we need to be creative and recognise that all professions have the potential to be compassionate. Think of the young football team that were stuck in a cave in Thailand in 2018. Scuba divers, geologists, psychologists, doctors and government officials were all working together to alleviate the suffering of those 12 boys and their coach. The different skills of these professions were all being used for compassionate purposes.

It is still worrying how poorly compassion is understood. Many see the core qualities of compassion as warmth, love and kindness. Even our psychological sciences continue to measure compassion in these terms.[20] But the core of compassion is courage and wisdom.

As a species, having a better understanding of how we decide to help those suffering will I think lead to a better world. Charles Darwin observed that those who were most sympathetic to members of their group were the most successful. The same is true for humanity. But given the global challenges we are facing, with growing rates of inequality, vaccine hoarding and weapon manufacturing, it is possible humanity could collapse under the weight of our own self-interest. In this context we see compassion is more than a warm hug. Compassion offers us hope to tackle some of the world's greatest challenges.

2

The things that move us

It is easy to believe that compassion works solely through our emotions. Imagine seeing someone suffering – perhaps a family crying and distressed after losing their house and everything they owned in a natural disaster – then imagine not being emotionally moved by the scene. Humans are almost always moved by stories of vulnerability and hardship. Suffering toys with us like a puppeteer with a puppet. It makes us feel, and these feelings motivate us to try to help.

In a moral psychology conference this concept was taken to the extreme. At the conference, about 500 people were given their own robot dinosaur, called a Pleo. Pleos are as helpless as week-old babies and the conference attendees were told to feed and care for their small charges across the day. Then at the end of the conference the organiser announced that someone had to come on stage and decapitate their Pleo with a sword. If nobody volunteered, they would kill all the Pleos. This caused significant distress, with one person finally volunteering. Many at the conference were horrified that such an act could be both suggested and performed. Was it even ethical?

Let's remember, a Pleo is inanimate. But sometimes our emotions move us to act in ways that are perhaps disproportionate to the suffering witnessed.

In the example at the conference the attendees anthropomorphised their Pleos. People do this all the time. Try giving your pencil a name, say Sarah, and now snap Sarah in half. This makes most people slightly uneasy, despite the pencil being an inanimate object. Our emotions play with us even when there is no need for them to. Even when we don't want them to.

Our emotions can also pull us in two directions. A good example of this is a client I had called Beth, who was caught in some family tension. Her parents were happily married for 40 years, then tragically her mother died of cancer. About two years later her father got remarried to a woman a lot younger. Beth's brother, Chase, was livid. He didn't understand how their dad could have remarried so quickly. On the other hand, Beth felt sorry for her father. He had been sad and lonely, and she could see his new partner made him happy. In the end, Chase confronted Beth, not understanding how she could pretend the marriage was fine, while he thought their dad was an idiot for marrying 'some bimbo'. Since then Beth and Chase hadn't spoken, and she didn't know how to repair the relationship.

Beth conveyed in therapy that she understood why Chase was so angry. The grief over their mother was still so raw and present. And this new person, their stepmother, someone about their age who they were still getting to know, had just been thrust into their life. She had empathy for both her father and her brother and didn't want to lose either, but felt she was being pressured by Chase to choose a side and stop being 'Miss Nice'. This is a false dichotomy. We can feel empathy for both people in a situation without choosing who is 'right' or 'wrong'. That is a different question, a moral question. Many scholars argue that we should not rely on empathy as our sole guide for moral decision-making. Instead, this example raises the issue of zero-sum thinking, which is the belief that one person's gain is another's loss. We tend to view life competitively, and when we have arguments about things we can get caught up in the idea that we have to win, because we don't want to lose. If we were to put it in terms of two-player poker, my win of $50 is your loss of $50.

People often mistakenly apply zero-sum thinking to compassion. There can be a sense that I can only have empathy for one person in a situation, and anyone else must therefore be in deficit: if I give my empathy to Dad, then Chase must go without; there is not enough empathy to go around. Yet there is: my empathy can be a positive sum. Another way to avoid zero-sum thinking is to use our cognitive strengths and move beyond the narrow lens of 'me' in the interaction, and begin to consider the possibility of what can benefit 'us'. We can think our way through it, taking both perspectives, looking for possible mutually beneficial resolutions.

While you'll often hear the words 'I just felt like I had to do something', it isn't as common to hear 'After thoughtful deliberation I decided I had to do something'. This second pathway to compassionate behaviour is a cognitive or deliberative pathway. While the emotional pathway works extremely well for people we are close to, it doesn't work so well for out-group members, and this is where the cognitive pathway can be more helpful. The emotional pathway can put the blinders on to other perspectives and experiences, closing us off from being curious about other information. This is what was happening for Chase. He could only see the actions of his father and sister as betrayals of his late mother, who he was still grieving, causing him to feel animosity towards his father's new wife. He was so emotionally charged he was losing his last remaining family relationships.

We need to work with both our emotional and our cognitive pathways if we want to increase our compassionate behaviours. Neither pathway is more 'correct' or, perhaps better put, 'accurate'. We have both, and it is naïve to think we can base our compassionate decisions solely on logic without interference from our emotions. That being said, we also need to learn how to recognise the way the emotional pathway skews our decisions towards those we like, and work with this effectively instead of denying or suppressing it.

I might be jumping the gun here a little bit, though, as these kinds of nuanced points are based on the premise that we are a compassionate and helpful species. But do we really help that often? Aren't we just selfish?

The truth is, we help people so often, with so much energy and enthusiasm, that the media considers it boring. They don't show the millions of acts of compassion that occur every day. For example, we donate to charities to help people we will never meet. In 2016, an estimated 14.9 million Australian adults (80.8%) gave in total $12.5 billion to charities and not-for-profit organisations.[1] The average donation was $765. According to the World Giving Index, in 2020 more than 2.5 billion people had helped a stranger in the last decade, and globally nearly a fifth of all adults volunteer.[2] Blood donations to the Red Cross are another good example: in 2020 around 1.5 million donations were made in Australia alone. Some of us, perhaps the most altruistic, even donate kidneys.[3] In 2020, 182 people in Australia were living donors; that is, they donated their kidney to save another person's life while still living themselves. That's extraordinary compassion. Taken on average that means every second day of the year a person is donating their kidney to somebody. But we don't see these kinds of compassionate acts on the front page of the newspaper.

These compassionate everyday actions give us hope. In some ways they can even make us proud to be human. If we based our assessment of humanity solely on the news it would be a bleak report card. One study found that watching the news significantly deteriorates mental health.[4] The 6:00 pm bulletin only reports the negative, the worst. Why? Because it is rarer, not the norm.

My field of psychology has also done its part in trying to convince everyone that at our core humans are bad. In his seminal book, *Humankind: A hopeful history*, Rutger Bregman does a comprehensive job of dissecting the many problems of the psychological research that has shown the evils of humankind. He examines the three classic studies held up to demonstrate that humans are more bad than good: the bystander-effect study, where nobody came to help a young woman stabbed in a busy New York neighbourhood; the Milgram shock experiments, where people gave a lethal electric shock to a stranger for making a spelling error; and Zimbardo's Stanford prison experiment, where ordinary students (assigned to be 'guards') treated other ordinary students (assigned to be 'prisoners') so badly the study was ended prematurely. Each of these studies seemed to support the idea that humans are no good: apparently we don't help each other (bystander), we hurt each other when told to (Milgram), and when given a role we embrace it even if it means causing harm (Stanford prison).

One of the problems with the studies mentioned above is that they were done in the 1960s and the laboratory notes were classified and couldn't be accessed. You couldn't do this today. All experimental procedures used in psychology need to be open, transparent and available, so that others can replicate the experiments. Beyond this, Bregman draws upon a significant body of work done in the last ten years that sheds light on the problems these studies tried to hide. And what he reveals is that humans are often the exact opposite to what these studies have led us to believe.

For example, the bystander effect is a phenomenon where we don't help others when we believe someone else will. The study led people to believe that they would be better off having a heart attack in the presence of just one person than a crowd. But researchers have found there is more nuance to this. There are times when this bystander effect does hold; for example, when we think others will do a better job, when we are afraid to help, or when we don't think anything is actually wrong. But if the situation is an emergency and bystanders can communicate with each other, there is actually an inverse bystander effect. More people lead to more helping. Researchers used CCTV footage in the Netherlands to examine moments when people needed help. The conclusion: 90% of the time when it's needed, people help.[5]

When it comes to Milgram's shock experiments, research has found we aren't obedient when told to do harm. Rather, when given a direct order to shock a victim, participants refused every single time. The video recordings and transcripts of the study also show Milgram and his experimental team were forceful and bullying towards participants, urging them to press the shock button. Another striking finding is that only 56% of the participants in the experiment believed that the shocks they were administering were real.

However, it isn't all rosy for us humans: many of the participants in Milgram's experiment still delivered what they believed were painful shocks. And these results have been replicated by other research teams around the world.[6] According to Professors Alexander Haslam and Stephen Reicher, though, participants administer these shocks because they trust the experimenter.[7] In Haslam and Reicher's words: 'the participants do it because they identify with the person instructing them in the experiment'. Another take on it is that many of the participants follow the instructions because it's for the good of science. Remember, they were volunteers and wanted to be helpful. In the Milgram experiments, many participants expressed doubts about the possible harm they were inflicting while they were administering shocks. But their trust in the almost extreme utilitarian mindset of 'for the greater good' pushed them to continue, in the belief the scientific process would lead to important breakthroughs to help humanity.

Bregman describes painstaking research done by Dr Matthew Hollander, who identified the three ways that would reliably stop the Milgram shock experiment: the participant talks to the victim, the participant reminds the experimenter of their responsibility, and the participant repeatedly refuses to participate in the experiment. Do these three tactics sound familiar to you? When discussing what compassion is, I put forward the idea that the core of compassion is the qualities of wisdom and courage. These qualities are at the core of the tactics used to stop the harm of the experiment: having the wisdom to ask the victim how they are, and the courage to question the experimenter and stick to the principle of compassion.

Finally, in the Stanford prison experiment, some participants were assigned to be prison guards and were trained and encouraged by the experimenters to be harsh towards the other participants, assigned as prisoners. We were led to believe the guards became 'evil' because of their assigned role. Instead, scholars have analysed the tapes and transcripts of the experiment and found that Zimbardo and his research assistants were quite active in encouraging and instructing the guards to be harsh towards the prisoners.[8] When the guards objected, they were pushed harder by the experimenters.

The Stanford prison study is deeply flawed and has yet to be replicated. Haslam and Reicher in an attempted replication achieved results that were the complete opposite to the original study.[9] The participants in their study weren't told what to do, rather they were just assigned their roles as either prisoners or prison guards and placed in the cells. What did they find? That the guards and prisoners acted nicely towards each other, eventually becoming friendly, and questioned the experiment, which eventuated in the set-up being transformed from a prison to a larger group community. Like the original Stanford prison experiment the study had to be prematurely ended, but this time because the participants were too kind to each other. As it turns out, humans can be nasty if pushed, but really we try to be helpful where we can. Nevertheless, the message that 'humans are evil' sells.

The television and movie worlds profit from this false belief. Take the series *Westworld*, in which humans pay large sums of money to visit a created world where robots are indistinguishable from humans. In this world the humans live out their ultimate fantasies – for the most part involving sex and violence. We aren't shown a single character that goes into Westworld wanting to be compassionate: becoming the doctor they always dreamt of becoming to save lives, or joining a movement to liberate a stigmatised and prejudiced minority. But our compassion for the robots as viewers is stirred constantly as we see the shocking things done to them. We see their vulnerability, and it *feels* unjust. Despite knowing they are robots, viewers can't help but feel for these 'creatures'. Here the powerful emotional pathway towards compassionate action works its wonders yet again.

The emotional pathway to compassion is the primary pathway activated in daily life. We don't have to think about being compassionate to our children; our compassionate responses to them work off instinct. So much so that the care a parent has for their crying newborn baby is often used as a symbol of compassion. The parent holds the child, rocks the child, sings to the child and feeds the child, trying to comfort their distress. It is believed by some scholars that compassion emerges from this essential parental caregiving strategy.[10] The science is clear: parenting that is warm, responsive, secure and predictable is what sets children up for a thriving life.

Therapeutically, however, relying on these feelings to act compassionately is a significant problem. One of the most awful aspects of depression is the lack of emotional experience it creates. Someone with depression will no longer feel joy doing something they used to love. This terrible part of depression is referred to as 'anhedonia', which basically means loss of feeling. Not only do depressed people feel a total lack of energy and increase in negative emotions like frustration, they also lose the experience of positive emotions. It is a double whammy. One of the most empirically supported treatments for depression is something called 'behaviour activation', which essentially is about getting the person to start doing things.[11] Thus, rather than waiting to feel like doing an activity, they are encouraged to just do it, like a scheduled appointment. Doing the activity then leads to positive emotional experiences, and over time this reduces the severity of the depression. This is easier said than done, however, which is why working with a psychologist can be really beneficial. We have found that self-compassion helps people through this process, too, as it can aid the person with depression engage in activation, which reduces depressive symptoms.[12]

One profound therapy experience I had was with a mother who was experiencing postnatal depression. Her name was Mary and she felt alone, exhausted and deeply ashamed. Mary had recently had a baby girl, Louise, and at the time of Louise's birth Mary reported being extremely happy. She had always wanted a girl. However, not long after leaving hospital and arriving back home something changed. Mary was crying a lot, was feeling overwhelmed, had no energy and couldn't think. Worst of all from her perspective, she no longer experienced a sense of warmth for her baby. In fact, she felt no connection at all. I remember her saying, 'Mothers aren't supposed to be like this. There is something wrong with me. I shouldn't be a mother.' Yet the very reason Mary was in therapy was because she wanted to be able to do what she felt she was supposed to as a mother. To me this is an example of heroic compassion. Mary was depressed, and depression robs you of your emotions and leaves you feeling hopeless. Yet Mary was trying to find ways she could improve her health so she could be there for Louise so she didn't suffer. In Mary's own suffering, all she could think about was being there for her baby.

This example also shows that compassion is not an emotion. Mary wasn't experiencing warmth and feelings of love for her child, yet she was motivated to act so that she could prevent her child's suffering. And, after months of therapeutic work, those feelings of warmth returned.

This moment in therapy compelled me to do further work examining how we can help mothers who experience these kinds of difficulties not long after childbirth. I teamed up with some other researchers and we developed a brief online self-compassion intervention for mothers who had gone through some kind of unexpected traumatic birth experience. We found the self-compassion intervention helped mothers by reducing symptoms of post-traumatic stress, while also improving breastfeeding experiences.[13]

What is key to success in families and communities is the support from others around us. Some researchers suggest that the key number for social communities is about 150–200 members.[14] In communities of this size our emotional pathways to compassion help us respond to each other when distressed, as we know each other, and the wellbeing of each member of the group is important for the wellbeing of the community. This harks back to Charles Darwin, who famously posited that it is those communities with the most sympathy for its members that will best flourish and succeed. In other words, compassion is why our species continues to thrive and be successful. In times of human catastrophe, we see this time and time again.[15] We come together to help each other, showing remarkable compassion.

However, our communities have grown exponentially in recent times. We pass thousands of people just on the way to work, many of whom will speak a different language to us, look different, dress differently, eat different food, listen to different music. This diversity is what makes life so interesting and amazing, and why many of us crave travel. But these differences can act as a powerful barrier to emotional compassion. A study we did found that when being compassionate to those we know and like, we experience far fewer negative emotions (e.g., disgust, anger, fear) and more positive ones (e.g., joy). Yet when it comes to doing those exact same compassionate acts to those we know but dislike, we experience significantly more negative emotions and fewer positive ones.[16]

Humans have a hard time trusting out-group members. That is why we cannot rely solely on our emotions to help. In fact, the differences between us, often magnified by media discourse, can lead us to fear and dislike other groups. And although we have come a long way in understanding and accepting the many forms of diversity human life takes, there are still massive barriers to be overcome. For example, in the US in the 1960s people were surveyed and asked how comfortable they would be if their child married someone belonging to an opposing political party, with only 5% indicating they'd be displeased. This grew to 33–45% in 2010.[17] Unfortunately, in some areas of life we are seeing each other increasingly as out-groups, spotting the differences as opposed to similarities. Magnifying these differences and falsely pitting them against each other erodes emotional pathways to compassionate behaviour.

That is why we need a different pathway. It is our only hope to develop the often harder form of compassion: the compassion for people we dislike.

3

Thinking our way to compassion

We can't be compassionate to all if we rely solely on our emotions. But, fortunately, humans have incredible cognitive capacity. This is what makes us capable of deliberative compassion, where we step outside our own experiences and imagine the world from the position of someone else. In this way, we can choose to use our morals and ethical principles to guide our compassionate behaviours.

One unique human quality that enables deliberative compassion is mental time travel. To the best of our scientific understanding, other animals do not have the same mental cognitive capacity as humans (although we are finding out more and more about the extraordinary mental and cognitive capacities of other animals all the time). Humans on a regular basis will project themselves into the distant future or the distant past, and use that information to make decisions in the present moment.[1] Here is an example of mental time travel that I often use in therapy:

> Imagine you've reached the end of therapy. You have addressed the core problem you have come in with successfully. What are you seeing yourself doing differently in this imagined future? Knowing this future, and coming back to the present moment, what advice would you like to offer yourself to help you on this journey?

Here we have someone aware they exist in the present, the past and the future. The person then imagines what they might be doing, thinking and feeling in a range of different possible outcomes in the future. The person takes this imagined future knowledge and comes back to the present moment to provide advice to themselves. This exercise also shows we have the capacity to empathise with our future selves – and with others. We can imagine what this future self feels, thinks, and does.

Drawing on this cognitive skill, a study asked a group of people who were experiencing depression to be their own therapists and give themselves advice to overcome their difficulties. Another group of people, also depressed, were asked to imagine that they were Sigmund Freud and give themselves advice. Patients gave themselves better advice when they imagined themselves as Sigmund Freud and their mood improved significantly as well.

Not only can we do this mental time travel for ourselves, we can do it for others as well. In fact, we do this all the time when buying gifts for people. We know if we are buying a present for a friend, it is better to buy something they like than something we like. This is a seemingly simple cognitive task that we perform easily. But if we break it down it is remarkable. We imagine a future possibility (a friend being happy) and then think about what we might be able to do in the present moment to achieve that. The idea is to buy them a gift, but not any gift – a gift we know they will like. So that requires us to remember their preferences or imagine ourselves as them in order to work out what might make them happy.

This is all linked to theory of mind. Theory of mind simply refers to the ability to attribute mental states (e.g., beliefs, intents, desires, emotions) to oneself and to others. We don't always get things right, but theory of mind offers a window into imagining and creating future possibilities that might have a desired effect.

Studies intimate that humans can typically represent up to five orders of embedded theory of mind. Here is an example: you, the reader, *believe* that I *suppose* that you *know* that I *want* you to *believe* that compassion is good. A perhaps richer example of the five levels of cognition is the following:

> For the rest of my life {level 5}, I will look back on my past {level 4} and regret the fact that I failed to anticipate {level 3} that I would regret my past decision {level 2} to commit that crime instead of not committing the crime {level 1}[2]

43

Non-human primates (chimpanzees, gorillas, orangutans) aren't able to consider the future and its many varied alternatives in the same way we can. They also can't deliberately choose to reflect on the distant past – which may inform present-day action. Research has also found that chimpanzees find it difficult to imagine and prepare for alternative futures.

In an ingenious experiment, Dr Jonathan Redshaw and Professor Thomas Suddendorf asked children and chimpanzees to complete a task of uncertainty.[3] Catch a ball that is dropped down a piece of pipe tubing (about 60 centimetres long) that gives way to two openings at the bottom (a forked tube). The ball would come out on either the left or right opening at the bottom. The task was simple: catch the ball. The children were rewarded with stickers, while for the chimpanzees the ball was replaced with a grape they got to eat. From four years old, children recognised the uncertainty in the task and reliably covered both ends of the pipe with their left and right hands, ensuring success either way. The chimpanzees, however, only ever covered one end of the pipe. Even after a hundred trials, the chimpanzees never covered both ends to guarantee catching the grape.

Predicting alternative futures is something we do all the time. The gambling industry makes billions of dollars out of this. In chess, individuals create strategies by drawing on past examples and learnt expertise to anticipate what their opponent might be thinking and planning. Powerful computers are programmed to beat chess masters, and yet humans still win those games regularly.

We start to develop this capacity to imagine and prepare for uncertain futures at around four or five years old,[4] although in some cases we can get stuck. Clinical disorders such as anxiety and depression are examples of this. When one is depressed it is almost impossible to imagine a future characterised by hope, freedom and joy.

Mental time travel therefore presents us with a skill that we can use compassionately. In times of suffering we can ask ourselves, 'Is this something I want to avoid experiencing in the future?' If the answer is yes, we follow that up with, 'What can we do to make this future possibility a reality?' Again, take COVID-19 as an example. Our scientists went to work immediately to create vaccines to help prevent mass suffering. We had dedicated teams around the world examining different combinations and approaches to vaccination, and we didn't know which one was going to be the most successful. There were just too many unknowns. Now we have several vaccine options that are being used across the world to protect us. We didn't put all our eggs in one basket. We were able to branch off into many possible future scenarios in which one vaccine approach might not work, but another could.

Often our compassion is limited to those we know and like, but the deliberative pathway to compassion allows us to use mental time travel for compassionate means. So how do we go about extending compassion beyond our traditional boundaries? Work I have been doing with Dr Charlie Crimston addresses this. Charlie developed a measure called 'the Moral Expansiveness Scale' and it assesses the extent to which we view a range of entities as worthy of our moral concern. These entities range from people close to you, like your mother; to those not so close, for example a sick child with cancer; to those viewed as being 'bad' people, like a bully, criminal or terrorist. The measure also assesses our views towards animals, plant life and even inanimate objects.

The scale was inspired by Peter Singer's work on 'the moral circle'. The premise is we have this imaginary social boundary, and we believe people inside the circle are worthy of our concern while those outside are not. Where this boundary sits will vary from group to group, relationship to relationship, and person to person. There is research indicating that across history our moral circles are expanding.[5] Indeed, over the last 150 years the abolition of slavery, the recognition of women's rights and recently the recognition of same-sex marriage have increased our moral circles as a society, but we still have a long way to go and much to do.

Charlie has been doing research to examine what factors predict a morally expansive mindset at the level of the individual. That is, what makes you more likely to view others, regardless of who they are or where they come from, as being worthy of your moral concern. What is the key candidate that immediately springs to mind? For most it is empathy, and it does indeed play an important role, with higher levels of empathy predicting an increased morally expansive mindset. Other factors that predict a morally expansive mindset include endorsement of universalism (e.g., equality), and identifying and connecting with nature. Charlie and I have found that compassion also plays a crucial role. Even when you account for empathy and mindfulness, compassion is more predictive of a morally expansive mindset. But it is more nuanced than this. What we found is the most important predictor to one's moral circle is one's *fear* of compassion. That is, if you fear giving compassion to others you have a smaller moral circle, and this factor is more important than any other predictor to a morally expansive mindset. The reason? Many people fear that being compassionate to other groups means less resources for themselves. And this blocks them from including others in their moral circle.

The core message here is that our moral and ethical principles can overcome our fear of compassion and guide us to compassionate actions. I am reminded of this time and time again in therapy. There are moments when patients reveal things that they are ashamed of, things that society stigmatises. But as a therapist, if I am going to engage in compassionate help with this patient, I need to override my emotional response and recognise that this person needs connection. This is liberating, and leads to questions like, 'What happened in this person's life that led them to be violent towards a stranger?' It is a cognitive process that takes training, but it enables me to stay present so I can be an agent of therapeutic change. There is a saying in trauma and forensic literature that 'hurt people tend to hurt people'. What is paramount here is to recognise that the patient, the person, wants to change, and I want to help them with that, to try to stop the hurt. Shaming and punishing are not effective motivators and encouragers to positive behaviour change. Compassion offers a completely different opportunity.

A group in Portugal are doing cutting-edge research using a model of therapy called 'Compassion Focused Therapy', which was developed by Professor Paul Gilbert, to help people under 18 years of age who have committed a crime. The researchers are examining an intervention called 'PSYCHOPATHY.COMP' to help reduce psychopathic traits such as lack of remorse, impulsiveness, grandiosity, manipulation, callousness and lack of emotion. We tend not to be emotionally moved when individuals with psychopathic traits suffer, and the approach to such individuals is typically to exclude them from society. But it is clear that individuals with high levels of psychopathic traits need help. They suffer, as do the people around them.

The group in Portugal conducted a randomised controlled trial (which is the highest standard of evaluation for an intervention) exploring the potential of this compassionate approach. The study included 119 male detained youths aged between 14 and 18 years. The participants were randomised to either the PSYCHOPATHY.COMP program – 20 sessions, delivered individually, aimed to increase compassion – or a treatment-as-usual condition, which was 20 individual counselling sessions delivered by psychologists (an alternative and effective intervention approach). The compassion program was significantly more effective at reducing psychopathic traits compared to the treatment-as-usual condition, and this improvement was maintained at a six-month follow-up. This kind of result is almost unheard of.

Earlier I mentioned how generous we are and how we donate millions to charity. Unfortunately though, we tend to donate to charities we are affected by and thus feel a connection to.[6] The drawback here is that some groups receive more money than others because more people are affected by them. Donating money to charities is a personal decision, and the question of whether to give to a group that saves more lives or has more personal impact is difficult to resolve. That is why it is common to merge emotional and deliberative pathways to compassionate behaviour. I have isolated them, but we are often moved by suffering (emotional), and then we think rationally about the best ways to help (deliberative).

Take healthcare professionals. They may be *emotionally* moved to help those who are physically, mentally or socially suffering. Thus, they make the *rational* decision to spend years training to become a nurse or a social worker, for example. They deliberately choose to spend time, money and energy to become better at helping people in the future. It can also occur the other way around, where someone recognises that morally they have a responsibility to help a certain group of people, maybe refugees or detained youth, and then they direct energy towards helping this group, getting emotionally moved along the way.

How do we strike the right balance? This is the million-dollar question. Maybe it is better to think about this in terms of the 'level' of compassionate action. In our individual interactions in everyday life, we are mostly reliant on our emotional compassion. It tends to work reliably, automatically and quickly. Even in small groups, with families and close friends, it works well. However, if we take it up a level and think of a larger group, say an organisation like a school, or even government, the deliberative pathway becomes more important.

Extremely difficult decisions are made at the highest levels of government, as finite resources are funnelled to support one group of people over another. Take the decision of who we vaccinate first. Those decisions are not easy. Based on their outcomes, some people will continue to suffer – even die – and others will be saved or protected. These decisions can cause outrage in the community. The emotional pathway can easily cloud our judgement and lead us to subconsciously favour groups closer to us rather than leading us to what is morally right, fair and just. Equally, however, if we are too 'objective' at these higher levels, too far removed from the suffering experienced, we can lose the human connection and forget what it is like for individual people. They become numbers, and numbers can be sacrificed.

If we get to the heart of it all there is no clear way to be compassionate in all settings all the time. We simply try our best. Certainly, we can improve the way we are compassionate, and programs can do this, but there will be times when we favour one group over the other, and that's not our fault. We are human, and unfortunately we are susceptible to these things. Fortunately, we have scientists dedicating their lives to exploring how we can better balance these emotional and deliberative pathways.

Given the state of the world, it's important to remind ourselves we are a deeply compassionate species, perhaps even unknowingly. Not many of us wake in the morning with the intention to cause harm to people we meet that day. Being kind to each other tends to be the default setting; it shows we care for others and think of them positively when they aren't around. This helps build and strengthen our social connections. Interestingly, we also report finding altruism more attractive than good looks and a sense of humour.[7] Why? It suggests that in times of need, our partner will be there to help us. That is a deeply desirable trait.

Compassion isn't new to humans. Archaeological records suggest that early humans took care of injured and sick individuals, with evidence of dental care and splints for broken bones. Some researchers have posited that such caring behaviour gives us our humanity.[8] We create compassionate cities; in Medieval times the inner circle of the city centre was where the poor lived, as this meant they had access to the church and health care. Since then, many countries have deliberately developed some form of public access to health and education for all citizens, further strengthening the sense of compassion we have in our societies.

If we leave compassion to chance it will show itself most frequently to those close to us and not so regularly to others outside that circle. Deliberately choosing to be compassionate can take time, but it offers us the opportunity to extend compassion beyond our typical moral boundaries. Unfortunately, the early stages of life can do much to block the development of our compassionate motivation. But given we have the unique capacity to have large-scale compassion that extends to other species, in some ways we have a responsibility to harness it so that everyone can benefit. Imagine having a superpower but never using it. Fortunately, many of us do.

4

Compassion in the family

When you reflect on your childhood and think of your parents, what are the three words you would use to describe them?

When I ask this in therapy I sometimes hear 'warm, loving and encouraging', and that sounds like just the kind of environment you'd like a child to be raised in. More often though I hear 'stressed, critical and busy', and maybe 'They were trying their best, though'. There can be a strong feeling of guilt when a patient describes their parent in negative terms, so there is a tendency to try to correct it or balance it. Sometimes they might even say, 'Yeah, but I was a little shit.' My follow-up question is usually 'When you were upset what did you do? Who did you turn to?' In the former situation the answer is always the parents, in the latter typically 'Nobody'. Or you might get 'I tried not to show it', or 'I don't know. I guess I just worked it out on my own.'

Being raised in a family where the parents are stressed, critical and busy is less than ideal, but a common experience. Unfortunately, some have a much worse time of it. These experiences in early childhood are critical to how we build relationships, trust others, and learn to give and receive compassion. A major study that followed 2761 children over 30 years found that greater levels of emotional warmth from parents in childhood predicted greater levels of compassion in later life.[1] Put simply, the quality of the parent–child relationship matters for compassion. The family, particularly our early childhood experiences, can lay the strong foundations that make compassion easier for us in later life.

There is a huge body of work that shows that the best way to set children up for a positive life is to raise them in family environments that are safe, predictable and warm.[2] Being compassionate to the distress of one's child is at the core of parenting. One study I did found that parents with compassionate parenting goals were more likely to engage in warm and responsive parenting, while those focused on their own self-image (wanting to be seen as 'right' or the 'perfect' parent) were more likely to be controlling and critical of their children.[3] Parenting styles are strong predictors of childhood social, emotional and behavioural outcomes, with facilitative (warm and responsive) parenting leading to better outcomes, and controlling parenting being detrimental for children.

Today, if you do a Google search on parenting you will be met with millions of articles on what to do and what not to do, with terms such as 'helicopter parenting', 'tiger parenting', 'lawnmower parenting', 'bulldozer parenting' and many others now part of the vernacular. I find it striking that there is so much advice available on parenting. What did parents do before the internet? Or before the advent of self-help books?

I suppose one reason for the sheer amount of parenting advice available today is because how we raise children has changed from when we lived in small hunter-gatherer groups. People in these smaller groups would get to know the child, protecting it and at times offering comfort. This is commonly referred to as 'alloparenting', a phenomenon where the care of children is given by individuals other than the parents, which is usually but not always close relatives.[4] In these communities the relatives and other group members were present 24/7 to help with child-rearing. Children were able to roam freely and could seek contact, comfort and play from whoever they chose. This is still the case in hunter-gatherer groups today.[5]

There are a few vestiges of this way of living and child rearing in Western industrial society. For example, in most Western societies one in four grandparents are involved in regular childcare.[6] Other non-parental care certainly exists, but this is commonly provided by strangers for allotted periods of time such as formal childcare support services, nurseries and schools.[7] Some research has found that cortisol (a stress hormone) increases over the course of the day when a young child is in formal childcare versus when the child is at home with a primary caregiver[8] – an important caveat to this of course is the quality of the care given.[9]

In hunter-gatherer societies, co-sleeping, open breastfeeding, ease of touch, and open expression of affection by kin and non-kin alike are part of normal everyday life.[10] This is hugely important, as we have vast amounts of scientific evidence that shows physical contact is one of the most powerful affect regulators to create a sense of safety and comfort.[11] A powerful illustration of this is kangaroo care for premature babies. This is a method of holding a newborn baby on the chest of the mother or father with skin-to-skin contact. The baby is secured by wrapping a blanket or robe around parent and baby, which looks like a mother kangaroo holding her baby in her pouch. The method was developed by Edgar Rey Sanabria in Bogotá, Colombia, in 1978, when the death rate for premature babies was extremely high. Research has found kangaroo care reduces infant mortality, improves physiological regulation and helps with sleep and breastfeeding. It also helps relieve procedural pain for mothers and improves neurodevelopment of the child.[12] It is recommended as the standard of care for all infants around the world. Parents describe kangaroo care as one of the most powerful things they've experienced, creating an incredible bond with their baby. Only a hundred years ago fathers weren't even permitted in the delivery room, and not long after birth the baby would be put in a crib, sometimes in another room, separate from their mother. No other primate in the world would be okay with that. What were we thinking?

A consequence of our modern social context is that many families live separately from their naturally occurring alloparenting groups, such as grandparents or aunts and uncles. In Western cultures we live in separate houses, often in different suburbs, cities and countries. This freedom of movement is tremendous, but it is not without cost. One of the major consequences of this is loneliness and disconnection, which is a serious issue in Western countries such as the US, the UK and Australia.[13] Loneliness is associated with a range of mental and physical health problems,[14] all of which are likely to impact on child rearing. One study recommends that if you want to be happy, have children, but also live close to your family.[15] In the context of parenting, a recent survey of 2000 mothers found that 90% felt lonely since having children and 54% felt friendless after giving birth, and single parents are at a heightened risk of loneliness and isolation compared to parent couples.[16] We are seeing a shift from supportive alloparenting communities to more isolated and vulnerable parenting.

Some scholars argue that the future success of humans as a species relies on returning to cooperative breeding and alloparenting. The way modern societies are structured, though, does not make such a transition easy. One advantage of returning to a more alloparenting lifestyle is it releases the burden of parenting on single individuals. There are many single parents, most commonly single mothers, living with significant stressors and systemic prejudices that make parenting extremely difficult.[17] Alloparenting also enables children to receive warmth and care from other adults, which is particularly important if their own parents are the source of threat or dysfunction. In alloparenting communities, the patients I see today who had nobody to turn to when they were upset as a child would have had a grandmother or an uncle to run to so that they could receive some form of external regulation in the form of warmth and care. That's not to say alloparenting resolves everything, but it affords parents the support and connection that so many are desperately wanting, as evidenced by the number of parenting books being sold. The books are meant to fill the gap, but a page can't touch you, or say, 'You're doing great.' Hearing those words from somebody you love is immeasurably more powerful than reading them in a book.

One study demonstrated the impacts of touch and voice on stressed and upset children. The study was focused on seven-and-a-half-year-old children and their mothers. The experiment required the children to complete extremely difficult exams, exams that they could not pass. After failing the exam the child was randomised to one of four conditions: be comforted by their mother in person, be comforted by their mother over the phone, be comforted by their mother via text message, or be left alone. When the mothers comforted their child they had all been told to say the same thing. The study measured the child's comfort in those four conditions by measuring reductions in cortisol and releases in oxytocin.

What the study found was remarkable: when the child was able to be with their mother in person or speak to their mother over the phone, cortisol significantly reduced, and oxytocin was released. Text messaging their mother and reading her text response did nothing.[18] The impact was the same as when they were just left alone. Striking. Our bodies are simply designed to respond to touch, smells and vocal tones. Text messages have none of that.

Researchers have noted that Western cultures have drifted away from raising our young in supportive groups and are instead raising them in increasing isolation. Large numbers of parents have also moved away from practices such as co-sleeping and extended breastfeeding. Such changes have been called an evolutionary mismatch, meaning that our ecological and social context is now radically different from what our brains and bodies evolved to operate within.[19] Parents are more likely to feel isolated and negatively judged by others when in public with their children, while children are living in a sea of strangers. When they're distressed, their teachers are not allowed to physically touch them to offer comfort.[20] More concerning is the possibility that parents are unaware of typical child behaviour, thus interpreting typical behaviour as problematic.

I ran a series of Compassionate Mind Training seminars for self-critical parents as part of a large randomised controlled trial with over a hundred parents taking part. As part of the seminar we would spend a moment reflecting on the following question: 'Before becoming a parent, how much time did you spend with children in daily life?' Some had gone years between seeing children. Given the average age of becoming a parent today is early 30s, many have gone over a decade without daily contact with children by the time they become a parent. There are of course exceptions, such as schoolteachers, childcare workers or paediatricians. But for the vast majority of us the fact of the matter is that for years we don't really spend any daily time with children. There are some massive implications of this: we don't see how children tend to develop, we don't see how other parents and adults engage with children, and we lose about a decade of time playing with children.

Playing is such an important part of life. It helps with creativity and is fun, but as adults we are so focused on getting things done that we don't play. In fact, we forget *how* to play. Evidence for this disconnection between adults and children is illustrated in a report about 2200 parents, which found that 36% of them thought children under the age of two should have enough self-control to resist something forbidden. Yet this skill does not develop until ages three-and-a-half to four. Moreover, 42% of parents believe children should be able to regulate their own emotions before age two.[21] I find this striking, as it seems in some ways we have forgotten what it means to be human.

This brings us to the next question in therapy. 'Now, as an adult, when you are upset what do you do? Who do you turn to?' The responses typically include 'I work it out myself', 'I bottle it up', 'I download a meditation app', 'I might go for a run', 'I more often than not have a drink' or 'I eat'. Some of these help in the short term, no doubt about it. But clearly they are not as effective in the long term, because people are still turning to professionals like psychologists for help. Turning to someone for help is important, because it is a recognition that external sources can help regulate the difficulties of life. Having supportive people around you and receiving compassion from them is hugely powerful, but often we can leave it till we hit rock bottom before turning to others. Humans are a hyper-social species. We need others to help us flourish.

Another way to think about the importance of family as the building blocks of compassion is to contextualise humans as mammals and take a closer look at the mammalian parental investment strategy.

Animals have either r or k selection strategies for reproduction. Reptiles and fish are examples of the r selection strategy, which simply means having lots of offspring at once who, when born or hatched, disperse quickly. They are born mobile, seek their own protection and are self-sustaining. A sea turtle mother, for example, lays 80–120 eggs, buries them, then returns to the ocean, never seeing them again. When the eggs hatch two months later, the baby turtles emerge from the sand and scurry to the water. They are on their own. The baby turtle has everything they need to survive. The trade-off is that a baby turtle is incredibly vulnerable, and only about one in a thousand makes it to adulthood (these odds used to be higher prior to human industrialisation). However, this strategy has been successful for turtles for over 110 million years.

In contrast, mammals have the k selection strategy, which means having few offspring at a time and investing years into that offspring so that it reaches adulthood. As a result, the child relies on their parent for protection and sustenance, and the parent and child need to stay close to aid the child's development.

Researchers examining parent–child interactions in monkeys and humans have found secure attachment plays a crucial role in healthy development. This refers to the relationship between child and parent, where the child is soothed by their parent after they have been distressed. Insecure attachments are those in which the child is unable to be soothed or comforted by their caregiver. Secure attachments have been found to be strongly predictive of good mental health.[22]

Attachment is important in mammals. When a child is distressed not any adult will do to help soothe them; one specific adult is sought out and needed, the one with the strongest secure attachment (usually mothers or fathers). Often mammalian young will stay with the parent for two years. In the case of humans, we need about 10–15 years, although many in the Western world now stay with parents until they are 25–30. During this time, the parent protects, feeds, teaches and cares for the offspring so they can become independent and self-sustaining. A huge amount of parental investment, but it has been successful for mammals for millions of years.

One of the key functions of parental investment is to have sensitivity to distress in one's young and a preparedness to act appropriately to relieve that distress. This, of course, is the core of compassion. Mammalian young send distress calls (cries) that prompt parents to respond, which might involve providing warmth via holding and touching, singing, or maybe providing shelter or food. The child finds such acts comforting or relieving. A distressed baby turtle, on the other hand, isn't going to be soothed by touch, as it doesn't have the physiological infrastructure to do so. Mammals do. Joeys, for example, need the warmth of being held constantly. It aids their growth and development. For human babies, touch helps myelinate the vagus nerve, which is connected to various internal organs and is critical to good physiological health.

Dr Harry Harlow conducted a landmark study into these important physiological processes, in which orphaned baby monkeys were given access to either a 'mother' figure that was made out of a cold wire frame but provided food, or a figure that was warm (a cloth covering the wire frame) but provided no food. All the baby monkeys forwent food for the warm figure, such is the significance of warm attachments. And when they were deliberately scared by the experimental team, the monkeys always ran to the cloth mother. However, what a terribly unethical and un-compassionate study, to deprive baby monkeys of the warmth of a proper caregiver! The devasting effects on the monkeys were never overcome. As adults they never felt safe with other monkeys, showing severe deficiencies in social and parental behaviour.

Research shows that physical contact in parent–infant relationships is critical in fostering a feeling of safety, which is important for continued psychosocial development.[23] Research with young bonobos (our closest primate relatives) reared by their mothers shows they are more likely to exhibit consolatory or empathic behaviour compared with orphaned bonobos.[24] Physical contact between infant and caregiver characterised by warm emotion is critical for mammals. When we get it, we thrive; when deprived, we suffer.

Countless studies have demonstrated that children raised in warm, responsive family environments grow up substantially better off than children raised in cold, critical, sterile environments. At its worst is the case of the Romanian orphans during World War II who were given basic food and shelter, but were starved of contact. These children, who experienced this severe deprivation early in life, had smaller brains in adulthood.[25] Our brains grow more outside of the womb than inside, so the environments in which we are raised impacts how our brains develop, and the functional connectivity between regions of the brain. Moreover, being held, kept warm and spoken gently to, as well as receiving facial expressions of warmth and caring, have multiple positive physiological impacts on the maturing infant.

Despite the importance and power of human touch, and affection being a crucial physiological regulator, 50% of parents in Australia still smack their children as a form of punishment. Smacking occurs across all socio-economic backgrounds, from poor to rich.[26] In a study from the US in 2009, 10% of parents self-reported using smacking with an object on a frequent or very frequent basis. Critically, meta-analysis (the highest form of evaluative evidence in science) has found there is no evidence that smacking does any good for children and all evidence points to the risk of it doing harm.[27] Some countries, like Sweden and New Zealand, have banned smacking – indeed, over 40 countries have.

A core problem with smacking is the children on the receiving end can begin to see their parents, who are supposed to be sources of safety and protection, as sources of threat. When smacked by the parent, where does the child go to regulate the experience? Smacking in some cases can also lead to potential problems with physical abuse and harm. Parents can smack in anger and cause significant damage. There are so many other effective strategies to help children when they are struggling.

If smacking happens regularly, children can begin to blame themselves for being a 'problem', believing they deserved it. Nobody deserves to be hit. One of the core principles of compassion is to prevent suffering, not cause it. Often when a child is struggling they show this by yelling, screaming, running or hitting. We can easily label this as the behaviour of a 'difficult' or 'challenging' child, but these are actually signals for help. You could even describe them as compassion-seeking behaviours, enacted consciously or unconsciously. The child's suffering is being shown in unpleasant and unskilful ways, but compassion isn't about pleasantness. The compassionate algorithm is simply: see a signal of suffering, help alleviate it.

Unfortunately, though, there are millions of children throughout the world who are maltreated and neglected. According to the World Health Organization, the three major risk factors for child maltreatment are: the child being under four years of age; the child being unwanted; and the child having special needs, crying consistently or having abnormal features. What is the key theme here? Vulnerability. These children desperately need compassion, yet their vulnerabilities make them targets for further punishment.

Thankfully, there are a number of parenting programs that teach positive parenting practices to help parents nurture their children. Many of these programs are delivered by the World Health Organization and other not-for-profit groups to help support children by giving parents effective and positive parenting information. State governments in Australia over the last five years have also made accessing parenting support free. Parenting is not easy; we all need help from time to time, and one of the best investments we can make as a community is in helping parents to help raise their children, as that sets them up for a thriving life.

There is no doubt that parenting is challenging, but it is also incredibly rewarding, with many saying it is the greatest thing they have ever done with their lives.

In my early research days I looked at the role of grandparents in family life. I interviewed many grandparents who were heavily involved in providing regular childcare to their grandchildren to get a sense of how they found their role, and the overwhelming response from them was that it gave them a chance to parent again, but this time with more wisdom and more joy. Of course, for some who were giving huge amounts of care it was also exhausting. In Australia there are over a million children who receive regular childcare from their grandparents.

Better parent–child relationships, characterised by emotional warmth, are a good predictor for compassion in adulthood. Parents' levels of compassion also predict how they respond to children. In one study, researchers had mothers and their three-year-old children in the lab, and the children had to complete a task, one an age-appropriate puzzle and the other an origami task.[28] Origami is very challenging for a three-year-old. The mothers were told they could help their child, but only through verbal instructions. They couldn't physically assist.

What they found was in the difficult tasks, some mothers got frustrated when their child struggled with completing the origami, which was expressed in their voice, in negative facial expressions and even in their physiology, which shifted to a stressful state. These mums would even take the origami off the child and complete it themselves. The mothers' levels of compassion, as determined by a self-report questionnaire, predicted this behaviour in the experiment. A low score on the compassion measure predicted negative responding, whereas mothers high on the measure fared more positively. It appears that compassion helped those mothers in a difficult parenting situation, enabling them to avoid stress-induced aversive parenting. Put another way: compassion can prevent us from causing inadvertent harm.

I am doing work now examining how compassion might be a source of help for parents and children. I mentioned the Compassionate Mind Training seminar we did for self-critical parents. We found that we were able to significantly reduce self-criticism and increase self-compassion in the parents and reduce child emotional and peer problems.

In a separate study, where we included compassion modules in a parenting program, we found significant improvements in child prosocial behaviour.[29] We were very excited about this, as many parenting programs are focused on reducing problematic behaviour in children, but not many have been found to work.

Another study found something similar, but this time while looking at childhood generosity.[30] In this experiment children completed a range of tasks and would earn tokens that they could later exchange for a prize. Before they exchanged their tokens the experimenters told the child that they could donate some of their tokens if they wished to other children who were sick in hospital or having a hard time. The researchers did this study when the child was four and then again two years later when they were six years old. They found that children donated 25% of their tokens when they were four years old and 20% of their tokens when then were six. Overall, the pattern of generosity was stable across time, such that children more generous at four were more generous at six. Moreover, the mother's level of compassion, measured again using a self-report questionnaire, predicted the generosity in the child. The researchers concluded by stating that if parents want to nurture their child's compassionate instinct, they need to show them compassion when they're struggling. The child's experience receiving their parents' warmth and tenderness will prepare them to extend care to others in turn.

Another study that aimed to help stressed parents was conducted using a program called 'Cognitively-Based Compassion Training'.[31] In this study parents were randomised to either receive the compassion program or to a waitlist control condition, which means they were given the program at the conclusion of the study. To determine if the compassion program was effective at reducing stress, the researchers measured cortisol in the parents and children both before and after the program. What the study found is that the program did not reduce the cortisol levels of the parents, but it significantly reduced the cortisol levels in the children. This is a significant finding. Compassion can help improve the physiological stress experienced by children.

We did a study to see if we could help mothers in the first 24 months post birth adjust to their parenting role using self-compassion exercises. Over 250 mothers completed the study and we found that the program helped increase self-compassion, reduce post-traumatic symptoms from childbirth and improve subjective breastfeeding experience as well as overall satisfaction with breastfeeding. Moreover, the vast majority of mothers (98%) agreed that self-compassion was helpful for women experiencing birth or breastfeeding difficulties.

In another randomised controlled trial we found that the inclusion of a compassion module in a parenting intervention led to significant improvements in the parent–grandparent relationship. Specifically, we found the compassion module led to increases in parental self-compassion, but also to a reduction in conflict between parents and grandparents in their co-parenting relationship, as well as improvements in prosocial behaviour in children.[32]

The family matters for children and it also matters for the development of compassion. But it is important to recognise that it is okay as parents to make mistakes. We can't get it right all the time. Unfortunately, some parents place incredible pressure on themselves and criticise themselves when they do make mistakes. And that is why we ran the Compassionate Mind Training program to help those parents who tend to be self-critical. Because all parents have times when they do something they regret later, like yell, make threats or call their kids names. In these times, they need self-compassion. They need to remember their basic goodness, that when they wake up in the morning they aim to try their best. It is critical to recognise that mistakes happen, but rather than ruminate over them, we can try to repair them. We always have an opportunity to press the reset button.

This was really well demonstrated in a study called 'the still-face experiment', conducted by Professor Edward Tronick and his team.[33] In this experiment the mother engages with their infant, looking at each other, being connected and being in tune with each other, like a dance. Then the experimenter instructs the mother to sit for two minutes with no facial expression, simply looking at the infant with a still face. When the mother does this the infant immediately picks up on it. The baby tries to re-engage the mother by smiling, pointing and making noises. When this doesn't work the baby tries all manner of things to get the mother's attention back, calling out, screaming, starting to cry and even losing body posture. After the two-minute period the mother is instructed to re-engage again with the baby. The baby extremely quickly goes back to the friendly interactions of before, back into the rhythm of the dance. The experiment shows how responsive we are to non-verbal cues. Importantly, the mother doesn't even have to pull an angry or hostile face to make the baby feel distressed. A neutral face is all it takes.

We find neutral faces very threatening even as adults. Why? Because we don't know what the person is thinking or feeling. What is really important in the still-face experiment is the reconnection, because we all make mistakes like this in our parenting, when we don't see or hear our child because we are focused on something else, say our phones.

Tronick frames the message of the still-face experiment as a representation of the good, the bad and the ugly. The good is the day-to-day normal parenting interactions you see, such as the interactive dance between mother and baby, and that sense of connection. The bad is the disconnection. But this can be repaired, when the mother comes back to the baby. The ugly is when that repair work is never done. The mother doesn't press reset; she doesn't go back. The child is left alone.

I have focused primarily here on the impact of compassion and parenting on young children, as research shows that what a child experiences in the first three years of life is very important for their ongoing mental health and wellbeing.[34] I have also discussed a lot of parenting and compassion research for children under 12 years of age. However, the family is also important for adolescents. During the adolescent period, the key attachment figures in the child's life transition from parents to peer group. Compassion plays an important role here as well, but less is known about it.

One study did report a remarkable finding in American adolescents aged 15. The study was conducted at Harvard

University and is called the 'Making Caring Common Project'. The study surveyed 10,000 adolescents across the US and found that 80% said 'achievement or happiness' was their top priority, compared to 20% who said 'caring for others' was their top priority. Moreover, the study found youths were three times more likely to agree than disagree with the statement: 'My parents are prouder if I get good grades than if I'm a caring community member.'

In contrast to these findings, research indicates quite clearly that parents say they want to develop caring children as a top priority, as they see it as more important than school achievements.[35] However, this message does not seem to be filtering through to their adolescent children. There is, as the report puts it, a glaring gap. What do we do about this? Obviously there is no simple answer, but in Western societies that are characterised by individualistic cultures and pursuits, it is hardly surprising that adolescents are prioritising self-interest before others. It is not their fault. What these findings highlight is the kind of communities and environments we are raising our children in, and what they reward. For example, right now affluent countries all over the world are reducing foreign aid to countries that desperately need it, under the mantra of 'me first'.

There is an important role for school-based educational programs to help encourage compassion and caring behaviour in children and adolescents as well. Research has found that self-compassion buffers adolescents from stress,[36] and compassion-based programs can improve levels of self-compassion in teens.[37] However, the role the family plays in nurturing and supporting compassion in adolescents isn't so well known. We need to do more work here. Unfortunately, adolescence is an oft-neglected area of research within psychology, despite this period being textured by huge transitions, uncertainties and difficulties in our lives.

What we do know is, if children aren't exposed to a warm family in childhood, as a grown-up they can come to fear compassion. And fears of compassion can cause a range of mental health and interpersonal difficulties.

5

Fears of compassion

Humans are funny creatures; we can fear anything. We can fear success, failure, the dark, small spaces, insects, spiders, mice, snakes, heights, clowns and the list goes on. In psychology we describe a process called 'classical conditioning', in which two things are paired together, producing a specific response. A clear example of classical conditioning is the fear many people have of dogs. Many of us love dogs, humans' greatest companion (cats are okay), but as soon as we get bitten by a dog or a large dog runs towards us, this love turns to fear. What happens the next time we see a dog? We immediately feel that fear, and we want to avoid the dog, even if it's a pet we previously loved. This is an example of classical conditioning. Something that was previously liked, even loved, has now become associated with danger, so much so that we now want to avoid it.

This exact same process can happen for compassion. How? As it turns out, the process is very similar to how a fear of dogs can originate, but more often than not fears of compassion begin in the family. Paul Gilbert proposes that how we experience our parents in childhood is crucial in our development of fears of compassion. But to describe the process it might be best to share an example.

I had a patient who was struggling with depression. She was in her late 30s and her name was Angela. She was doing very well professionally, with a good network of support, but felt like she didn't really connect with anyone. At one point she said, 'I feel like I am just who people want or expect me to be, and never really just me.' After some time together it became clear that Angela was indeed an expert at being able to read what others wanted or needed. It was one of her strengths. She said it was one of the reasons she was successful at her job. But it came with a trade-off, because she was always attending to and thinking about what the people around her needed, and she would put her efforts into ensuring those needs were realised before her own. When we dug a little deeper, Angela shared that one of the reasons for doing this was it meant people needed her. It meant people would want her and like her. But Angela was left feeling empty. Because to her, the only reason they liked her was because she helped them get what they needed. If she stopped doing that, then those friends wouldn't be there for her; they wouldn't *really* like her.

I asked Angela when this first started, and she said, 'When I was a kid.' She told me about her family, and how her mum and dad did their best, but they seemed constantly stressed and were very critical. She said her dad's side of the family were very cold. She could recall times when her mum was quite loving, reading stories together at night as a child, and there were times she caught her singing. Her mother had a beautiful voice, Angela said, but she didn't like singing in front of people. The real source of concern was her dad, though, as he always seemed angry.

Angela remembered hurting herself pretty badly when she was about five years old. She had been playing in the garage and fell off the workbench. Her dad happened to walk into the garage as she was falling. Angela cut her knee in the process of falling, and she says, 'I didn't realise I was bleeding at first. All I remember was being scared. Dad was so angry with me for being on the bench that he yelled at me and smacked me on the bum for being a naughty girl.' I asked what she did next, to which she replied, 'I ran to my room crying.' At this point Angela became tearful. She said, 'Dad came to my room and he kept shouting at me to stop crying. I was too loud, and he smacked me again.'

This is an example of how a fear of compassion can originate. We expect our parental figures to be sources of protection, love, warmth and support. And when we are hurting, we expect they will be there to help us. In Angela's case, rather than being a source of compassion, her father was a source of threat and punishment. When Angela was seeking help and comfort from her dad, she was punished. So her sadness was paired with anger and punishment, which left her feeling not only scared but also alone in her room. Angela had quite a few memories of childhood that were similar to this. It wasn't a one-off moment. The repetitiveness is what was really damaging. And so in her adult life Angela often felt alone. When she was sad and hurting, she did not turn to others for help.

Angela said her dad was unpredictable at home. There were times he would be happy and laughing, and at other times he was angry, which was worse when he had been drinking. Angela was always keeping an eye on him, monitoring how he was feeling to make sure to stay out of the way if he was angry, or trying to find ways to make sure he wouldn't get angry. So Angela would do things around the house, like cleaning and tidying, or cooking on nights when her mum was out. She even made sure to play outside away from her dad so she wouldn't annoy him.

Angela's family environment had been her training ground for life, and the conditions involved a lot of unpredictability and anger. Everything she did was aimed to make sure others were happy and not angry so she wasn't hurt. This kept her safe, but it had a long-term trade-off. It meant Angela struggled to trust people. She struggled reaching out for help when she needed it, and she felt alone.

In one session, Angela confessed she felt ashamed that she needed to be in therapy. One of the reasons was because she felt like her problems weren't really 'bad enough' for her to deserve or need help. There were others in much worse situations. In

Angela's own words, 'I'm crying because I want to feel like I am Daddy's little girl, and I'm almost forty. I'm just an attention seeker and need to grow up.'

Such a statement is striking due to its complete lack of self-compassion. Angela was quite clearly suffering, and in that moment of suffering she dismissed her pain and at the same time attacked herself.

Despite some of these difficult childhood memories, Angela said her parents always supported her, particularly financially, and she said the 'tough love' she got from her dad made her push hard for things. Angela also recognised that one of the reasons she pushed herself in her work was to make her parents, in particular her dad, proud. She desperately wanted to hear him say she'd done well.

As a result of this family background, Angela had a tendency to fear compassion. She feared receiving compassion from others, and she feared being self-compassionate. One time in therapy I asked her, 'If your closest friend was going through this, what would you say to them?' Her response was, 'It's not your fault. You were only a child, and look at the amazing things you've done.' Clearly Angela had no difficulties with expressing compassion towards others. When asked if she could say that to herself, she started crying. She just couldn't direct that kind of compassion towards herself. She was scared of it and felt she didn't deserve it.

How do you know if you fear compassion? One way to work it out is to think about how you feel when people are compassionate to you when you are suffering. Do you feel open to others helping you when you need it? Or do you find it difficult? Many of us find it difficult. A common scenario familiar to any parent is being out shopping with your kids when someone offers to help. Often our immediate response is 'Thanks, but I'm okay', even when the help would make things easier. More often than not, we block the compassion. One reason is because we don't want to burden others. However, this action deprives them of the opportunity to be helpful. When we help others, we can feel really good about it. We experience a warm glow.

Another reason we often block the help of strangers is because we don't get a chance to help them back. We can feel a debt when we can't help a person in return. We do have the chance to pay the act forward though and give that gift of compassion to another stranger.

A final reason we can block compassionate help is because we don't feel we are suffering enough to deserve help. Many of us wait till we are desperate before we allow others to help. But getting help earlier is far better.

We all tend to have some fear of compassion. Unfortunately, like Angela, some people can have very high levels of fear, believing they are undeserving of compassion and that they will become weak and their flaws will show. Some believe that if they allow themselves to receive compassion from other people they will become too overwhelmed and upset.

In the movie *Good Will Hunting*, Will Hunting has to see a therapist, named Sean. There is a powerful scene between Will and Sean in the therapy room that shows fear of compassion very clearly. Sean is reviewing Will's case history, and there are photos of Will in which you can see the bruises on his body from the abuse he received from his foster dad. When looking at this, Sean tells Will that it wasn't his fault. Will immediately dismisses Sean's compassion, putting up a defensive wall. Sean, a skilled therapist, says it again, 'Look at me, son. All this, this is not your fault.' Again, Will dismisses it, not looking at Sean. But Sean keeps going, and after a period of silence says again, 'It's not your fault.' Then we start to see some cracks open in Will's emotional wall, as he starts to cry slightly, and with some anger begs Sean not to mess with him: 'Not you.' This is a plea to not be hurt again by someone he has become close to, who he has begun to trust. But Sean persists, and again says, 'It's not your fault.' Finally, the floodgates open, the tears flow and an outpouring of sadness is released – sadness that Will has supressed for years.

It is a perfect demonstration of fear of compassion. Will is fearful of receiving compassion from Sean, as he knows he will become intensely emotional, and he is scared of this vulnerability. But Sean knows Will needs to experience these emotions, especially in a safe environment, so that he can begin to process them.

In therapy we call this process 'exposure'. We expose individuals to their fears in gradual ways so that they can overcome the fear, but also so they can have a different, corrective, learning experience. In this therapy exchange Will is allowing compassion in from someone else for the first time in years. The experience brings intense emotions, but critically he is in a safe and supported environment. Nevertheless, it is risky for Will to allow compassion in and be vulnerable, because his entire childhood and family experience has been one of being hurt by people who should have protected him, and these memories stick.

The key message here is that family is a powerful context. It shapes our behaviours and our sense of self. If the home environment is characterised by hostility and, at its worst, abuse, it can lead to people fearing compassion. Angela had a fear of compassion. Will Hunting had a fear of compassion. And it wasn't their fault.

Paul Gilbert has done pioneering work in psychology examining fear of compassion. During a group therapy program he was running for those who experience high self-criticism and shame, many participants expressed fears and concerns about being compassionate, with some saying 'others have the power to reject and hurt me; they can turn nasty at any moment'.[1] As a result, these participants avoided moments of compassion. One fear was that if they allowed themselves to experience compassion from others or be self-compassionate it would mean they would emotionally break down. But why would this happen? The theory is that this kind of care and compassion is what the person has always yearned for, but for whatever reason they never received it. Consequently, a real grieving process begins as the person recognises how this care and compassion was never provided by those who were supposed to be loving and supportive, such as their parents, or maybe a spouse, sibling, aunty, uncle or teacher.

The program was a success. Participants had a significant reduction in feelings of shame and self-criticism, as well as a significant increase in their ability to be self-compassionate. At the conclusion of the program, participants were asked to reflect on their experiences and highlighted that the validation of their grief was extremely important for them, as they became more sensitive to their own distress when opening up to compassion. This feedback emphasises the importance of not rushing through the process, but allowing participants to open up slowly in the context of a safe therapeutic space, allowing compassion to be fully felt and realised.

Researchers have found that those who have memories of childhood that are high in shame and low in warmth and safeness have significantly higher fears of compassion. This is also predictive of greater psychological distress, in particular depression, anxiety and paranoid symptoms.[2] Unfortunately, as parents it is impossible to avoid all moments of shame our children might experience, and we can even shame them by accident. For example, a parent making a comment such as 'Oh please, you aren't wearing that, are you? Can't you dress more like your sister?' can be an experience of shame for a teenager. They can feel that their parent sees them as unattractive and not as good as their sister, devaluing them. And how we dress as teenagers can be an extension of our identity, so that is also part of the judgement. A teenager can easily think, 'What's wrong with how I dress? This is me. Why can't you love me for me?'

Shame is a complex emotion. It is what is called a 'self-conscious' emotion, meaning that it's based around how others might see us or feel about us. For shame, those judgements are all negative, such as 'I am bad' or 'I am seen as a bad person'. The behavioural consequence of shame is often that we want to hide or keep secret the thing we are ashamed about.[3]

In a Compassion Focused Therapy group I ran for those with body-weight shame, many of the patients said that despite loving swimming, they wouldn't go to the beach as they didn't want others to see their bodies. As one participant put it, 'Everyone thinks I'm a whale in swimmers.' As a result, the participants hide their bodies and don't go swimming, missing out on the joy and fun they would otherwise experience.

When I teach about shame, I ask people to bring to mind a memory of something they did that they are ashamed of and to think about it for a couple of minutes, asking them to remember the situation, remember what they did or didn't do, or what they said or didn't say. I ask them to open their eyes and turn to the person beside them, and then I ask them to share that shame experience. At this point, everyone in the lecture theatre gasps. I then say, 'No, it's okay. You don't have to.' At which point there is a collective sigh of relief. But I then ask them, 'If I did continue to gently push you to share your shame memory, what would you do?' The first response almost always is 'I'd lie!'

One of the core defences we have for shame is to hide it by lying. If we do share the shame memory a real fear is that the person who hears it will start to see us in a less positive light. They will see the 'real' us. That is a fear of compassion as well. We think that if we let others in to our pain, they will see the bad in us, and then they won't like us very much. Compassion is all about suffering, and many suffer with memories of shame. As a result, they fear compassion because that means letting other people know about their shameful acts, whether that is infidelity, gambling, cheating, drinking, bullying someone – and the list goes on. Many of us keep these secrets, not daring to share them with others.

There are times though when we do confide our secrets in others, but how do we decide who to confide in? This is a question that drove some research I did examining secrecy. Our hypothesis was that people don't just choose anybody to confide in, they choose people they see as being compassionate.[4] In our first study we asked people who they think they would ideally want to share a secret with. And then we asked them to complete a personality self-report measure that listed all the personality qualities of this ideal person. We found participants said they wanted a polite confidant and not an assertive one.

In our second study, we then asked people to complete the personality measure in relation to people they had actually disclosed secrets to. We found that people who were judged as compassionate and assertive had significantly more secrets confided in them, and those judged as polite had significantly fewer. Why? Because politeness means a person is much more likely to follow social etiquette and norms, and most of our secrets are violations of those norms. A polite person might judge you harshly for drink driving or cheating, for example. We also believe that when confiding a secret many people aim to get some resolution, and assertive people are willing to tell you ways to overcome the issue.

People often come to therapy because of things they are ashamed of, and these experiences will differ in intensity for people. I often ask patients, 'Does anybody know you've come today?' and commonly the response is no. There is still shame around seeking therapy, although I think that is changing with COVID-19, as we have all realised the importance of looking after our mental health. But it is impossible to stop all moments of shame. Given this, how do we stop our children developing fears of compassion? It turns out that although memories of shame in childhood make us vulnerable to fears of compassion, memories of compassion, safety and warmth from our parents protect us from the deleterious impacts shame can have in later life.[5] So if we can ensure that as parents we are, for the most part, responsive and compassionate to our children, this sets them up for a positive future.

But is there anything we can do to help those who have strong fears of compassion in adulthood? Meta-analytic work I have done with my colleagues with data from over 5000 people shows that those with high fears of compassion have higher levels of self-criticism, shame, depression and anxiety.[6] Having fear of compassion is a vulnerability factor for a range of painful experiences. So if we can reduce these fears this would be a very good thing. And the good news is, yes, there is hope. We can reduce fears of compassion.

How? There are many ways. One, as already mentioned, is exposure. Importantly, this doesn't mean just ramming compassion down a patient's throat, but gradually introducing it. Dr Russell Kolts has a good initialism for introducing compassion to those that might be fearful of it: SMST. The first step is to *Support it*, which is done by validating the fears of compassion the person has and de-shaming them. In the *Good Will Hunting* example, Sean saying 'It's not your fault' is an instance of de-shaming. Importantly, Sean doesn't say this once; he repeats it several times. The second step is to *Model it*, which is done by showing compassion with your own actions. Humans are the best imitators on the planet; if we see someone do something we will copy it. The third step is to *Shape it*, by validating when you can the person's wisdom and compassionate actions. In some ways we are reinforcing it, and this we know leads to more compassionate actions. Finally, the fourth step is to *Train it* with specific programs.

But can you train yourself to be more compassionate? Is that possible? That is what the next chapter unpacks.

6

Training compassion

I'm often asked, 'Can anyone really become more compassionate? Surely somebody like Donald Trump couldn't?' The short answer is, yes, anyone can become more compassionate, but to what degree remains uncertain.

If we all wanted to become like the Dalai Lama or Mother Teresa, for example, we couldn't. But, like all skills, if we spend time working on it, we can improve. The range of improvement will be different for everyone. Some will make huge improvements after only a little bit of practice – I am sure we can all relate to having friends who have taken up a new hobby or sport and become experts almost overnight – whereas for others it might take a lot of time and struggle to see even small improvements. A key ingredient in whether we develop a new skill is if we are motivated. But of course, desiring to become better is not the same as taking action to become better. You have to make time, prioritise, practise, seek feedback and watch others. Really, you have to make it a habit, a part of your daily routine. And forming habits is hard work.

Many of us start the new year in the same way, with a resolution, the most popular being to get fit.[1] How do we do this? For many it means getting a gym membership. But there are no compassion gyms to train in, so where and how do you train your compassionate muscles?

Many learn how to be compassionate based on their family experience. The famous golden rule, to treat others the way you wish to be treated, is one many families have. This philosophy underpins basically all the major religions. Many countries around the world have governments designed to support this premise, by having public housing, public education, public social support and universal health care. Many of us want to live in societies and communities that value and prioritise helping each other, particularly when we are vulnerable and need it most.

What is another avenue through which to learn compassion? One familiar to many would be meditation or mindfulness practices. At the touch of a finger, you can download one of hundreds of meditation apps that have compassionate mantras within them. A mantra is simply a phrase or a word that you repeat or concentrate on, the idea being that focusing on the mantra can lead to the cultivation of that wish or intention.

In many compassion meditations you might focus on a mantra such as 'May I be free from suffering'. Buddhist meditations focus on trying to cultivate what they call 'the four immeasurables': *friendly-kindness*, also known as 'loving-kindness', an intention of wishing others happiness and goodwill; *equanimity*, remaining calm and composed particularly in times of difficulty; *appreciative joy*, the feeling of happiness for others; and *compassion*, the intention to keep sentient beings free from suffering.

When practising a meditation like this, you direct your compassionate intentions through a series of stages to different targets. At first you ground your body through posture and breathing. Then you focus your mind through mindfulness to attend to the compassionate intention. You then take the next step of extending this compassionate wish to specific targets. First, you might direct your compassionate wishes to people you love, like family, your husband or wife, son or daughter. To make it more personal, it is good to say their names. Then, after sending your loved ones a compassionate wish, you gradually widen out and shift your focus to another target, such as a friend. And then you widen again to colleagues, then to acquaintances, to strangers, to a difficult person, and finally to all of humanity and sentient life. You can also direct this compassion towards yourself.

Research has found that these kinds of meditations are helpful at improving mental health and wellbeing.[2] And it isn't just one study; there have been many randomised controlled trials conducted, with meta-analytic evidence finding strong support for the effectiveness of these compassion meditations. Many therapies include such meditations as part of the therapeutic journey, such is the strength of evidence supporting them.[3]

One formal compassion-based program using this kind of approach is Compassion Cultivation Training. This program was developed at the Center for Compassion and Altruism Research and Education (CCARE) at Stanford University. I was fortunate to work there in 2016 after receiving a fellowship grant from the Australian government. CCARE received a significant financial contribution from the Dalai Lama to help set up scientific exploration into compassion training. His English translator, Dr Thupten Jinpa, was based there, and Jinpa developed the Compassion Cultivation Training program with a team of other Buddhist scholars and researchers. It is an eight-week program with weekly group sessions that span two hours. Each session has a specific focus, whether it be on attention training, compassion or loving-kindness. In each session you complete guided meditations and work with a partner where you discuss the exercises or moments you've had in daily life where you've been able to show compassion.

The Compassion Cultivation Training program has been evaluated in many rigorous randomised controlled trials and has been found to increase compassion, reduce fears of compassion, reduce mind wandering and improve emotion regulation.[4]

In Jinpa's book *A Fearless Heart*, he has a very interesting anecdote about the very first group he ran. In the original structure of the program participants were instructed to send compassionate wishes to themselves first, before widening their compassionate circle to others, like loved ones, friends and so on. But what they found was people were not comfortable with this. Jinpa found this interesting, because in Buddhism all deserve compassion. But there is a paradox in Western individualistic cultures, as we tend to find directing compassion to ourselves difficult, even though the focus is typically on 'me me me'. It is often much easier for people to start compassion meditations by focusing on other people, such as their loved ones, then finishing by focusing on themselves.

There are two important distinctions often made between meditations. One form of meditation is about becoming familiar with your own mind. This means you aren't cultivating anything specifically, but you are becoming more aware of the nature of your thoughts and attention. This is what a lot of modern-day mindfulness practice is about. There are many terrific books on mindfulness mediations, such as those by Professor Jon Kabat-Zinn, Thich Nhat Hanh and Sharon Salzberg. Often the purpose of mindfulness is to become more aware of your unfolding experience in an open and non-judgemental way: your experience of thoughts, bodily sensations, sounds, smells and so on. Mindfulness practice can involve open awareness, or it can zoom in on a specific thing, like the breath, or just sounds, for example.

If you anchor attention to the breath, the idea is to just watch it come and go. Your attention will wander off, but the aim is to simply notice this and bring it back to the breath. Nhat Hanh would say that mindfulness is remembering, remembering to always come back to the present moment. One very large study found that our minds tend to wander off to other things about 45% of the time, but importantly, our minds are most happy when they are focused on the thing we are doing, as opposed to other things.[5] As a result, people often try to do mindfulness practices to improve focus. Mindfulness can help us remember to come back to our compassionate intentions.

Many people have completed some kind of mindfulness-based retreat. A very popular one is a Vipassana retreat (often seven or ten days). The focus of Vipassana is to see things as they really are and to build insight. As such, the aim of this kind of meditation is to develop a much deeper understanding and awareness of the mind.

The other form of meditation aims to cultivate something specific. Many focus on cultivating specific attributes, such as loving-kindness or compassion.

Meditation and mindfulness are also practised in yoga. There haven't been any direct studies looking into the link between yoga and compassion yet, so I am currently working with Celia Roberts, a leading yogi in Australia, to examine these links.

If you don't really want to do yoga, go on a Vipassana retreat or become a Buddhist, there are other ways to help train and build your compassionate muscles. Over the last 20 years there has been a real explosion of work done in the compassionate sciences, and research teams have developed a range of compassion-based programs that are more secular in nature. These programs include the Mindful Self-Compassion program, developed by Drs Kristin Neff and Christopher Germer; Compassion Cultivation Training, developed at Stanford University; the Cognitively-Based Compassion Training program, developed at Emory University; and the Compassionate Mind Training program, developed by Paul

Gilbert. Each of these programs has a slightly different focus, but all aim explicitly to cultivate compassion. Importantly, there have been a number of randomised controlled trials conducted on all of these programs, and meta-analytic work done by myself and my colleagues has found that all of these programs are effective at improving self-reported levels of compassion, as well as improving overall general wellbeing.[6]

All these programs include some type of meditation, but there are also a range of other practices, including imagery exercises. These are exercises in which you are asked to close your eyes and imagine being compassionate towards someone. Imagery exercises are helpful because when we imagine things it activates the same neural regions associated with experiencing the sensation.[7] So we can begin to activate our compassionate muscles simply by imagining being compassionate. We use this imagery process all the time in therapy to help overcome fears. Critically, it is much easier to picture things with our eyes closed, rather than open, because the brain regions recruited for looking and imagining are the same.

Imagine taking a bite into a wedge of lemon. Think about the sensation of the acidic juice bursting out and hitting your tongue. Go ahead and close your eyes and spend a few moments imagining it.

How was it? Most people find when they close their eyes and do this that they salivate a little bit. The body is getting ready to take on the acid from the lemon. But of course, there is no lemon. Our body's physiology prepares itself even though it is all just fantasy. We can deliberately choose what we imagine, and if we imagine compassionate things it can help our bodies a great deal. If we imagine terrible things, it activates our stress centres.

So we have covered meditations and imagery exercises. What other things do you do in these compassion programs? For the most part all programs include grounding exercises – exercises to do with body posture and breathing. This is similar to how you would warm up when doing physical exercise. Breathing is part of the grounding process, where we purposefully start to control the breath. We might start with 'watching' the breath come and go, just noticing the sensations. But then we might transition into something more specific, like soothing rhythm breathing, which I use all the time. This is a breathing technique in which you slow the breath to a count of four to five seconds for the in-breath and four to five seconds for the out-breath. The key is to have a smoothness of the breath; you want to breathe slowly and at a steady rate on both the inhale and exhale, rather than breathing in and holding for the rest of the count. We focus on breathing to help steady the mind and body. It is much easier to activate a compassionate mindset from a calm frame of mind than it is in an anxious, fearful or angry frame of mind.

To give you a sense of some of the specific compassion practices you might be asked to do in these programs, I thought I would provide a couple of examples. This is not a self-help book and if you are struggling with stress or other difficulties, please do talk to someone or seek professional help. These examples are simply to give you an idea or a sense of what compassion training might look like.

One specific exercise we use in Compassionate Mind Training is called 'compassion in the morning'. This exercise includes four steps and takes no more than two minutes.

Step 1: When waking up in the morning try to connect to your breath. Then start to do one or two cycles of soothing rhythm breathing. This just takes a minute

Step 2: Welcome yourself to the day by saying hello to yourself using a friendly facial expression (a soft smile, perhaps) and with a friendly inner tone. You might say something like 'Good morning, James'.

Step 3: Take a minute to imagine what your day would look like if you were at your compassionate best. How would you talk to, feel towards and interact with other people?

Step 4: Try to do this morning routine once or twice a week to begin with and see how you go.

I introduce this exercise with almost all the patients I see, as it is such a helpful way to create a compassionate intention for your day. When we practise this in the session with patients, often there is a lot of laughing, which is really good. If you do these practices too seriously, they are less helpful. It is important to try to bring some playfulness and friendliness to the exercise. Many people with high levels of self-criticism or depression lose a sense of fun, through no fault of their own.

To demonstrate how welcoming yourself in the morning works I contrast the friendliness with a neutral facial expression and voice tone. So I would start with neutral, transition to friendly, go back to neutral, and finish with friendly. When reflecting on the exercise, patients almost always report that it's not till they have tried the friendly tone that they realise how 'heavy' the neutral facial expression and voice tone feels.

When I was doing this exercise with one group, a patient spontaneously said, 'When I welcomed myself in my neutral tone of voice I said, "Hi Rebecca," but when I did it with my friendly tone I said, "Hey Bex." I used my nickname that my friends call me.' When I asked her how that felt, she said it was totally different. She said, 'It felt like the "Bex" voice was super interested in me, but when I said "Rebecca" it was like I was getting into trouble from my teacher at school.'

Now these are of course just small things. And these things alone are not going to lead to transformative changes. But when you start to combine these little things together – tone of voice, friendliness, nicknames, breathing, posture, mindfulness, meditations and so on – it can start to make a difference. When we imagine ourselves in this friendly and compassionate way we stimulate the same regions in the brain as if someone was actually saying and directing this compassion towards us.

There is one other compassion exercise I'd like to share, called 'the ideal compassionate other'. In this exercise we ask people to close their eyes and imagine their ideal compassionate other. This other can take any form; for some it might take the form of an animal or even some vast landscape like the ocean. But for most people they will imagine some kind of person. When imagining your ideal compassionate other we suggest not thinking of someone you know, as that brings other memories and associations. For example, if that person has passed away it can be very sad. The idea is to create a completely new person, one perfect for you. You don't have to create a picture-perfect polaroid image of this person – that is not the idea of the exercise. The idea is to get a felt sense of what this ideal compassionate other might look like. You might not even get a clear sense of the image; it might be more of a fleeting feeling, but that's what we are aiming for.

If you were to do this, what would your ideal compassionate other look like? Would they be older or younger than you? Big or small? Would they be wearing glasses? How would they sound when talking to you? Do they have a smell? If so, what is it? Remember, you are creating this just for you, so create them the way you want. For me, I always seem to generate an Obi-Wan Kenobi kind of image, like Alec Guinness in *Star Wars*. But recently, my ideal compassionate other has changed to someone more my own age, and that has a completely different feel and energy for me. So the idea is to play around with it. Have some fun. Try older, then try younger. Try a man or switch to a woman. Be playful.

After creating a sense of the image, we then say this is someone you can turn to for help, for support, for encouragement or for whatever you need. This then leads to the next question: what qualities would this ideal compassionate other need for you to feel like you could do that? Often people need someone who is understanding, patient, calm, empathic, kind or compassionate. When we do this exercise, we always say that this ideal other needs the three specific qualities of wisdom, strength and commitment.

The wisdom part might mean that this ideal compassionate other has experienced what you have experienced. So if you are depressed, this ideal compassionate other has also experienced depression, but is now no longer depressed. Or if you are a single mum, they were a single mum, and have navigated that period of their life. This ideal compassionate other also recognises that we all find ourselves caught up in stress and worry loops, and they know this is not our fault. Their strength means that this ideal compassionate other can take and absorb whatever it is you want to tell it, while their final quality of commitment means they are always there for you, no matter what.

Now, given all this, what do you want to tell your ideal compassionate other?

This can be a very powerful exercise for people. I remember one patient, Amir, who I did this with. Amir was a young man who felt very insecure and was having some difficulty with his sex life, which was leading to levels of shame. Amir felt that he wasn't very good-looking and was worried his wife would leave him. So we created this ideal compassionate other. When reflecting on the exercise, Amir said, 'I told him what I was going through and how I felt. At first he didn't say anything back. He just sat down beside me, like we were on the side of the road together, and then put his arm around my shoulder.' At that point, Amir started to cry. He said when that happened, he felt like he was no longer alone with his problem. But then he said, 'I asked him what to do. And he just said, "Everyone has difficulties with their sex life, Amir. Things will get better."' I asked Amir how that felt. He said, 'Well, at the time when I was imagining it all it felt okay. But now, hearing it aloud, I kind of feel like he doesn't get it.' This is wonderfully insightful.

It can take time and practice to work out what this ideal compassionate other might say back to us to offer validating, compassionate and meaningful support. For some people, their ideal compassionate other knows the right things to say straight away, so it is different for everyone. The key idea though is that these exercises allow us to relate to our own difficulties in compassionate and supportive ways. They might not resolve the problem, but they can make things a little easier.

It's worth mentioning that many programs make a clear distinction between passive and active compassion. Passive compassion is our thoughts and wishes for a compassionate future; active compassion is taking behavioural steps to make a change. For example, you might wish that a certain group, say refugees, have a life free of suffering. Active compassion might mean volunteering at a refugee centre to help with tutoring, or offering some other kind of assistance to reduce some aspect of this group's suffering. Others will also distinguish between formal and informal compassion practice. Formal might be your ten-minute compassion meditation in the morning. Informal might be noticing how someone was compassionate to you in everyday life and then trying to do the same for someone else.

Compassion-based programs have been found to help with a huge array of problems, like mental health difficulties, loneliness and social connection, and self-criticism and shame. They can also improve a person's physiology.

But there is an elephant in the room. Do compassion programs actually lead to compassionate behaviour towards others? There are a few studies that have empirically tested this. One of the most well-known studies examined whether compassion training would lead to increased helping behaviour towards someone in pain using crutches. In this experiment, participants were randomised to either complete a compassion training course or were assigned to a waitlist control group.[8] The compassion training course was eight weeks long. At the end of the program the experimenters asked the participants to come back to the lab to complete some other cognitive tests. However, this was just a guise to examine the participants' compassionate behaviour.

When a participant arrived at the lab the experimenter told them to take a seat and that they would be with them shortly. There were three seats in the waiting area. Here the authors used confederates to take up the other two chairs, leaving one for the participant. Not long after the participant sat down, another confederate on crutches walked into the waiting area, visibly wincing and in pain. They had nowhere to sit. The aim was to see if the participant who had completed the compassion training would give up their seat. The study found that those who had completed the compassion training course were five times more likely to give up their seat than those in the control group. But still 50% of the people who did the compassion training did not give up their seat. So although we can improve our compassionate behaviour, there are limits.

You might be wondering why we don't do more behavioural studies like this. The major reason is because they need quite a lot of funding, and it is difficult to win grant money from funding bodies. As a result, it is much easier to ask people to complete surveys than it is to watch them in a behavioural experiment. However, these kinds of studies give us hope that we can make positive change.

An important caveat is that these kinds of interventions are all at the level of the individual. Sometimes the best way to facilitate compassionate help is to make structural changes. For example, if the cause of someone's suffering is poverty, making systemic changes like increasing minimum wage is much more powerful than a compassion meditation. Another avenue for change is creating superordinate goals. A superordinate goal is something that rises above the differences among people or groups.

We did a study on inequality where there were two groups: one with lots of resources to make food and another with very little. So a group of eight to ten participants came to the lab, and we assigned them randomly to either one high-resource 'country' or a low-resource 'country'. To avoid associations, we created two fictitious countries, Nasherland and Lindithia. We then read out information about the two countries to everyone, matching them on important descriptive information, such as having roughly the same population, having national sports, weather and cuisines. The idea of doing this is to help create a connection to the country assigned. This is done all the time in psychology studies; it is called 'using a minimal group paradigm'. It is an extraordinary effect: just assigning two groups different colours will lead participants to treat the others as out-group members.

In our study, we were attempting to create a United Nations-type scenario, with two countries trying to solve a world problem: hunger and starvation. The resources we used to create the food were represented by LEGO pieces, where the high-resource group had an abundance of LEGO, whereas the low-resource group had very little. Participants then engaged in a five-minute task where they were asked to assemble LEGO into food items to assure that 'no-one will starve'. We made this instruction clear, but ambiguous. We didn't say who the people were that were starving, and we didn't say what they could and couldn't do in the experiment. But clearly the more food made the better, as less people would starve. The high-resource group always had too many resources, so if they shared them with the low-resource group, more food would be made. If they didn't share, the resources would be wasted.

So how do you get groups to share? We tried two interventions to increase the likelihood of sharing. One was a compassion meditation. It did absolutely nothing. I of course was extremely disappointed by this, but it had no effect on sharing behaviour or the amount of food made. The other was a superordinate goal. We did this by planting a confederate in the high-resource group who would say, 'I think we should share with the other group.' This kind of intervention led to not only more food being shared but also more being created.

So it seems a more effective way to encourage sharing among unequal groups to solve social dilemmas, such as world hunger, is through superordinate goals: contributing to something bigger rather than relying on individuals doing compassion meditations.

Thankfully there are many avenues available to train our compassionate muscles. As I mentioned earlier, creating habits is difficult, so starting small is often best. Dr BJ Fogg, a habit expert from Stanford University, suggests the key to successfully integrating habits into daily life is to start as small as possible, pair it with something you do regularly (e.g., getting a cup of coffee) and immediately congratulate yourself for your effort with some kind of celebratory dance or 'woohoo' moment. According to Fogg, it is that emotional reinforcement that gets the habit embedded in daily life.[9]

One of my patients, Lorenzo, put this theory into practice. Lorenzo was having real difficulty with his partner, Jerome, whom he had been with for about five years. He said that they were both 'Type A' personalities, always working, and he said that in some ways it felt like they were in competition with each other to see who could work the most. One of the problems was they both worked from home, in digital technology, and it felt like they never unplugged from work. Lorenzo said he felt like they were drifting apart. There were just the two of them at home, they were always working, and it felt lonely. They didn't have the same intimacy as at the beginning of the relationship, and he was craving that feeling. He said they had spoken about this lack of intimacy a few times, but it always led to arguments. Lorenzo felt the gap was getting too big between them, and he didn't know how to close it. He joked once in therapy, 'What do I do, buy a puppy?'

Rather than buying a puppy, we decided to start small. And one small thing Lorenzo said he could do was each time he got up to make a cup of tea, he could walk over and give Jerome a kiss and make him a cup of tea as well. They both love tea, and would have at least five to six cups a day.

After a few weeks of this relatively simple action, Lorenzo said that the relationship felt completely different, for the better. He said the first time he did it, Jerome responded with, 'What are you doing?' Lorenzo said that the comment didn't feel great and he wanted to get angry about it. But he didn't. Instead he kept with his goal. And after about five days of doing this there was one time when he forgot to kiss Jerome while going to get a cup of tea, and Jerome said, 'Aren't you forgetting something?' It was at that point Lorenzo said he felt an energy, an intimacy between them that he hadn't felt in years. A few months later, for Lorenzo's birthday, Jerome bought him a beautiful tea set.

Small steps take a lot of commitment and they don't solve everything. But taking those steps is a fundamental requirement for creating change. Formal compassion programs can give you a helping hand at the start, but finding your own compassionate habits will play a big role in embedding compassion into your daily life.

7

The difficulties of self-compassion

When we think of compassion we typically think of people doing something to help another: someone attending to an injured stranger on the side of the road, helping a distressed colleague at work or listening to a dear friend who is struggling emotionally. All these examples involve interactions between people. At its core, compassion is a relational experience between two people, a group of people, or sometimes a person and another sentient being (e.g., a pet or a wild animal). There is an agent and a target of compassion. They can be individual-to-individual (from me to you) and group-to-group (a country helping another country), as well as individual-to-group (you donating to a charity), and group-to-individual (a family adopting a child). A beautiful aspect of this relational core of compassion is that it gives the target of the compassionate help the opportunity to feel what it is like to be seen as worthy of care.[1] This can be a very moving experience. The person can feel seen, heard and recognised.

Importantly, we can also extend this gift to ourselves, as the interaction between agent and target of compassionate help can be a self-to-self relationship. This is also known as self-compassion.

Many people find self-compassion difficult. Rather than being self-compassionate, they criticise themselves for their mistakes or failings. For example, they might call themselves an idiot or worse when experiencing a moment of pain or suffering. In Western cultures, it's common to believe that the function of this self-criticism is to help us improve at whatever it is we are criticising ourselves about.[2] A good example of this is dieting. Many people label themselves lazy, fat and ugly because they had a second bowl of ice-cream or ate the full block of chocolate when they were supposed to be on a diet. The rule is, *I must punish myself (with self-criticism) for this bad behaviour, otherwise I will never learn.* However, the science shows that self-criticism makes things worse,[3] and it is a major risk factor for depression and anxiety.[4] However, people often resist the idea of being compassionate in times of personal setback or failing.

When considering the idea of letting go of self-criticism and becoming more self-compassionate, my patients will typically respond with worries about letting themselves off the hook for mistakes they have made, or believe they won't improve and it will mean settling for mediocrity. They also worry about becoming arrogant and rude. These are classic examples of the misunderstandings of compassion.[5] The aim of compassion is not to make you rude or to lower your standards. Compassion addresses your suffering but equally encourages you with the challenges you encounter and helps you flourish and do better. Despite this, we tend to find self-criticism easy and self-compassion hard.

Let's take an example. When something goes wrong for you – say you get a job rejection, or you fail to keep up with your commitments, or maybe despite wanting to eat well you eat poorly – in these moments, how do you relate to yourself?

We did an experiment examining this. We gave people various scenarios and then asked them to either be self-compassionate or self-critical. We then looked at how their brains responded when being compassionate or critical to setbacks or failures.

Dr Jeffrey Kim (my PhD student at the time) was running the experiment, and he noticed something extraordinary. He would give the participants the instructions, and they almost always asked him, 'Can you give me an example of how I would be compassionate?' He was never asked how to be critical. Criticism is something we have become accustomed to. It is automatic. But being self-compassionate is unfamiliar.

We tracked these participants over a period of two weeks. During that time, they were given a link to an audio recording of an exercise aimed at cultivating compassion. The website allowed us to monitor how often each participant listened to the track, and we encouraged them to listen as often as they could. As we suspected, those who listened more often received more benefit from it. Other researchers have also noted this dosage effect with mindfulness and compassion meditations.[6] But there is an important nuance to this effect; for the impacts of these practices to really land, researchers have found it is most useful to use the exercise when you *need* it.[7] This seems simple enough, but it is actually a very important finding.

When trying to add a new practice into their lives, most people will add it to either the beginning or the end of their day: before getting ready for work, or just as they return home. Often the practice (maybe a guided meditation on an app) is done in isolation, perhaps even in a quiet tranquil spot. Indeed, some create a calming space in their home for their practice. This makes sense, as it is more inviting to do a practice in surroundings that are peaceful as opposed to busy and loud.

I had a client who struggled with intense self-criticism and depression. Gary had created a wonderful routine of meditation. He was about 67 and his adult daughter, Lilly, had recently moved back into his home with her six-year-old daughter, Chloe. Gary was retired and had plans to renovate the house. Those plans were abandoned. Perhaps the biggest difficulty for Gary was not knowing how long Lilly would stay with him. Her marriage had just ended due to her husband having an affair, and Lilly was just barely keeping it together. Gary was beating himself up because he wanted to ask Lilly how long she planned to stay, but felt that question would be met with her accusing him of wanting to kick her out. Gary was ashamed for even considering asking, particularly as, prior to this, he had been upset that she wasn't spending much time with him. He thought he shouldn't be feeling like this and having these thoughts, which is why he came to see me.

Gary was loving spending more time with his granddaughter and they were getting very close, he told me. However, one thing that really stirred Gary up was noise and mess in his home. And six-year-olds are brilliant at both noise *and* mess. As a result, Gary was constantly on edge, and he was trying to block these feelings out – which unfortunately tends to make things worse.

This curious psychological phenomenon is sometimes referred to as 'the rebound effect', which is when we try to suppress or block out an emotion or thought, and then that unwanted emotion or thought comes back even more frequently. You can give this a go yourself. Try not to think about a pink elephant for 60 seconds. Odds are that you thought about the pink elephant and you did so pretty quickly. If you didn't think of the pink elephant, you may have kept yourself distracted by concentrating on something else, but that's hard to do for long periods of time. But also, how do you know you have succeeded in not thinking about the pink elephant? The only way to answer that question is to think about the very thing you are not supposed to think about. It is a set-up. When we tell ourselves we mustn't, shouldn't, or can't think of something it often makes it much worse. To compound matters we can then get upset, disappointed or critical of ourselves for not being able to block it out. That's not our fault, though. Our brains aren't designed to block out unwanted things.

To help Gary with this I directed him to mindfulness meditation, which research shows is effective at helping with increasing the acceptance of unwanted thoughts and emotions.[8] Gary said he found the meditation helpful, but there were still problems. He would wake at 6:30 am, go to his meditation room and sit and listen to a guided practice for 15 minutes. He told me it was his favourite part of the day. But as soon as he finished the meditation and went downstairs, he would hear his granddaughter making a racket in the kitchen. Lilly would not be controlling the situation as he'd like, and he'd know she wouldn't clean up the mess – that would be left to him – and then they'd be out the door and off to school. When I asked what the problem was, Gary's response was, 'They've ruined my bloody meditation. I was feeling calm after my morning practice, but then I walk into that. It's useless.'

In this instance, Gary's mindfulness practice was allowing him to escape the busyness, mess and noise of his home, and it was allowing him to relax. That is important and of course nice for Gary, but it wasn't the reason we were doing meditation practice. Mindfulness makes us more aware and accepting of our experiences – what thoughts we are having, what emotions and sensations we are feeling, and what our behavioural urges are – and once we become aware of these experiences we can then try to choose where we would like to go, rather than being a slave to our emotions. When I realise I am becoming angry, for example, do I want to yell and shout so the kitchen mess will be cleaned immediately? Will that be helpful? Mindfulness gives us that tiny but important space to be responsive, rather than reactive, to our problems. That doesn't mean it feels positive or will resolve the problem – but it provides us with a chance to choose to do something else, something that aligns with the way we would like to be. In Gary's case, it was intended to allow him to connect to his desire to be compassionate, which meant he could choose to be helpful as opposed to yelling at his daughter and granddaughter for not controlling the morning routine and mess in the way he wanted.

Sure, Gary still felt irritated by the noise, but if he let his anger run the show all he would see in his daughter's actions would be things that justified his anger – and he would miss all the other things going on. Like, for example, how every morning his granddaughter would run straight up to him and throw her arms around his legs for a big hug, screaming, 'Pa!' Gary didn't like the sudden loud noise or how Chloe's fingers would be sticky from the porridge she had been eating. But if his attention was only on that, he would miss the joy and love he would feel from his granddaughter's warm affectionate hug.

Gary's wife had died several years prior, so that hug was typically the only physical affection he would feel all day. He found that emotionally intense, because it reminded him just how much he missed his wife. So some of Gary's anger with the noise and mess was a defence against his feelings of grief and loneliness. It annoyed him that he hadn't gotten over his wife's death. He was angry at the cancer that robbed his wife of her life – their life. 'James,' he would say, 'let's face it. Right now, Lilly needs her mother, not me. She was great at this stuff. But I'm all she has, and I'm a grumpy old fart.'

Gary needed his compassion for those moments when he was struck by anger or sadness. But he would ruminate over his disappointment for the rest of the day, annoyed at himself for getting angry, and then would wait for the next morning to do his meditation practice. Although we don't know what Lilly and Chloe were thinking, we can assume they needed him. Gary's own criticism was leading him to believe the exact opposite.

Dr Marcela Matos has found that if you become aware of these moments of criticism and bring your compassionate mind to them straight away, it's validating and improves your mood, making you want to repair the situation – helping you take responsibility for mistakes.[9] This is such an important point, as many believe that being self-compassionate to your mistakes is letting yourself off the hook. This is plain wrong. When we deliberately switch to our compassionate mind, we don't run away from our mistakes or moral failings, rather we turn towards them and try to do better. But many of us are like Gary. After making a mistake or failing at something, we stay in the pain by ruminating and often wait till the next day to do something helpful, like a meditation. It's like we need to be further punished for our actions before we can start to consider helping ourselves.

Going back to Jeff's study, we measured how often the participants listened to the compassion meditation practice, believing the more the person listened to the track the better they would do, in terms of having greater self-reported levels of self-compassion and wellbeing, but also in their physiological health. There is some hype in the media around compassion and mindfulness practice, about how it can positively change your mind and body. In this study we wanted to test this idea. One way to assess the impact compassion practice has on the body is to measure the person's heart rate variability when listening to a compassion exercise.

Heart rate variability is a measure of the variation in the time between your heartbeats. Most people think that a heart rate of 60 beats per minute is healthy if those beats occur once every second. Turns out that kind of commonsense thinking is wrong. The heart changes its rhythm with each beat. This variation is measured in milliseconds (ms), but it is a crucial measurement of both our physical and emotional health.

If you think of a heart rate monitor that you might see at a hospital, you see the peaks of the beats as though they are occurring with a constant fixed rhythm. Really, though, they vary quite a deal between each beat. They aren't happening second by second, they occur at 941 ms, then 991 ms, then 892 ms and so on. We are completely unaware of these subtle changes, but they indicate our heart's ability to respond to different situations, such as stress, threat and recovery. Two people can have heart rates of 60 beats per minute, but one person can have high heart rate variability and the other low heart rate variability, and it is the latter who has poorer heart health. In fact, if you are at the hospital and about to give birth, the monitors will track the baby's heart rate variability.

If it drops, the doctors will perform an emergency caesarean, because low heart rate variability is a sign of impending mortality. That is how important it is to our health.

Heart rate variability is also a good indicator of the health of your autonomic nervous system. There are two branches within your autonomic nervous system: the sympathetic system and the parasympathetic system. Your sympathetic system is responsible for activating your body's fight-or-flight system when you are faced with a threat. You could be minding your own business and then there's a loud noise; you immediately jump and run away. That's an example of your sympathetic system. It operates before we have time to process what the source of the noise is, working on the 'better safe than sorry' principle. The threat signal – the loud noise – causes our parasympathetic system to drop out, allowing our sympathetic system to step in and save us from potential danger. This setting in the system means we have many false alarms, with the threat (loud noise) turning out to be a friend trying to surprise us or a child playing a game. Although the symptoms of beings startled – increased heart rate and quickening of breath – are unpleasant, in isolation they have a low cost. Evolutionary psychiatrist Dr Randolph M Nesse refers to this as the 'smoke detector' principle,[10] with some of us having more sensitive smoke alarms compared to others (think daredevils or extreme sports fans). As he says, the occasional blare when you burn the toast is worth it to ensure that you are warned about a possible real fire.

The parasympathetic system, on the other hand, is connected to our calming state and is known as 'the rest-and-digest system'.

When in this state our bodies are more relaxed, our breathing rates are slower, and our bodies can do important recovery work. One reason it is called the rest-and-digest system is that it helps direct energy to metabolising ingested food. In a state of threat and danger, our sympathetic system directs that energy away from digesting food so it can be harnessed for escaping from a threat. Obviously both functions are important, so we need flexible physiological systems that are able to respond to the contextual surroundings we find ourselves in.

If you didn't have a parasympathetic system your resting heart rate would be around 160 beats per minute, so an average heart rate of 60–75 beats per minute indicates your parasympathetic system is working. It acts as a break, slowing the heart down. That is why when you are anxious about something it's a good idea to slow your breathing down. Easier said than done. It can take quite a lot of practice to become aware of your breath and change it on purpose, but the breath is one of the few physiological mechanisms you can control. To make things slightly more complicated, the in-breath is more connected to sympathetic activation and the out-breath with the parasympathetic system. That is why in many meditations there can be an emphasis on extending the out-breath.[11]

Both the fight-or-flight (sympathetic) and rest-and-digest (parasympathetic) systems serve important functions for our bodies, and we need both systems working well to have good general health. In today's modern world, our sympathetic systems are constantly being triggered, not by immediate predatorial threats like a lion but most commonly from social threats, as many of us experience great fears of missing out. As a result, our devices are constantly turned on and by our side so we can keep track of emails, social media and the news cycle. Some would say the entire year of 2020 was a constant trigger of our sympathetic systems, with COVID-19, bushfires, floods, an economic recession and a presidential election to contend with. One study found that purposefully deactivating their Facebook account for one month improved the mental health and wellbeing of college students.[12] Not only did the authors find it improved subjective wellbeing, but they also found it increased offline activities such as socialising with family and friends. It isn't as simple as 'social media is bad for us', rather it is how we use these platforms that is important.[13]

In an interesting study, researchers examined the links between heart rate variability and our quickness to assign blame to others.[14] In the experiment, participants read a story about a negative event and were asked to imagine it was about them. In the first part of the story the main character (the participant) is called to the phone during a group meeting with their boss. The phone call is to tell them they have been selected for another part-time job that is very important to them. On returning to the group meeting, the main character (the participant) passes a note with the news on it to their colleague, José, who is sitting next to them. They ask José to read it when nobody is looking, then destroy it. However, after José reads the note, it reaches the boss's hands.

At this point in the experiment participants were randomised to one of two possible conditions concerning how the note ends up in the boss's hands. One was the non-intentional condition: 'José opens the note discreetly and is about to read it when his boss looks his way and grabs the note thinking it was addressed to him. The boss reads the note before José can do anything to prevent it.' The other half of the participants received an intentional condition: 'José reads it at once and then hands it on to his boss, commenting that you have something to tell him because you appear to have found work with another company.'

What the researchers found is participants were generally understanding in the non-intentional condition. But in situations of intentionality, individuals with higher heart rate variability made less extreme evaluations of the offender's blame compared to those with lower heart rate variability, which resulted in a reduction in anger reactions. That is, those with higher heart rate variability thought more openly and with greater perspective, coming up with other possibilities that could have impacted José's intentionality. And this had a big impact on the anger they felt.

What makes this study so fascinating is the story resonates so strongly with everyday life. There are many instances we encounter similar to this, where it appears on the surface that someone has intentionally or deliberately done something to hurt us and we become understandably angry and show it. But with time, and as more information comes to light, we realise that perhaps the person wasn't as intentional as we originally thought. Then we can experience regret, especially if we have caused damage to the relationship.

This raises the important question: is there anything I can do to improve my heart rate variability?

The good news is, yes, there is. There are many practices we can engage in to strengthen our parasympathetic system so it doesn't drop away so quickly when these kinds of threats emerge. This is crucial when we think about compassion, as it requires interaction with suffering. To interact with suffering we might need to be open-minded, non-blaming or able to see things from a different perspective. Our body's parasympathetic system enables us to do this. In evolutionary terms, when we hear a distress call it is often a signal to scatter, as a predator is close by or there is potential for harm (such as disease).[15] But many humans will turn towards a distress call as opposed to running away. Our body's parasympathetic system allows us to think about possible causes for a threat and possible actions we can take to be helpful in the threatening situation. It is a crucial evolutionary design feature, as it means when we hear the distress calls of our young, we turn towards them and care for them. Not only mammals do this, but even crocodiles will respond to the distress calls from their hatchlings on the riverbank.

So, as a rule of thumb, higher heart rate variability is indicative of higher parasympathetic nervous system outflow, which is associated with increased feelings of contentment, calmness and safeness. Lower heart rate variability, however, is associated with the fight-or-flight response.

In Jeff's experiment, we thought the compassionate practice would strengthen the participants' parasympathetic systems and we would be able to see that improvement in increases in their heart rate variability. But why would compassion help with this? Lots has been written about these links. Work by people like Dr Stephen Porges[16] and Drs Julian Thayer and Richard Lane[17] has found that the body's parasympathetic system is strengthened through things like care and compassion.[18] Indeed, Porges even wrote a book chapter on how the vagal pathways are portals to compassion.

Across our development from babies to children, adolescents and adults, our autonomic nervous system, specifically our parasympathetic system, goes through a process of methylation, where the vagus nerve (the tenth cranial nerve that interfaces with the parasympathetic system) is strengthened if a child is raised in a loving and nurturing environment. The vagus is referred to as the 'wandering nerve', as it wanders from the brain to the vital organs throughout the body, via the neck, chest and abdomen. The vagus is responsible for the regulation of the functions of these internal organs, such as digestion, heart rate, respiratory rate and many other things. The methylation of the vagus helps us to function both physically and mentally.[19] It is a biochemical process in which a molecule called a 'methyl group' (one carbon and three hydrogen atoms) is added to another substance, such as our DNA, RNA or neurotransmitters (e.g., dopamine, serotonin). These newly methylated compounds then allow our bodies to function well. If the vagus is not methylated, our health – including our DNA and RNA synthesis and repair, immune system, and gene and hormone regulation systems – can be compromised and we can experience ill health.

Many scientists, not that long ago, believed that once we reached our mid twenties, we couldn't change our brain or our genes, as they were 'hardwired'. However, scientists in the 1970s and 1980s realised that this was wrong. Our brains can change across our lives through a process called 'neuroplasticity', and our bodies can change through the process of epigenetics. The methylation cycle is part of epigenetics. Methylation strengthens our genes so our bodies can function well.[20] Importantly, the environments in which we are raised have a significant impact on this methylation process.[21]

As mammals, humans thrive best when we receive affection from our primary caregivers when we are distressed. Being held, touched, sung to and spoken to all help calm and regulate a baby. This process helps in the methylation of the vagus and strengthens the parasympathetic system. Babies do not have the capacity to self-regulate their autonomic nervous system, so it is done externally, by their parents. Over the course of our lives we continue to be regulated by others, whether we like it or not. It is a crucial design feature. How others in our environment relate to us often becomes the way we internally relate to ourselves.[22]

Those who haven't received an upbringing with warm, safe and secure parenting often have over-dominant sympathetic nervous systems. They are also particularly self-critical, and tend to struggle with or even fear positive affiliative and friendly behaviours from others in times of distress. Indeed, research has found that children and young adults who report high levels of criticism from parents show significantly less compassion towards themselves.[23] And the ability of adults to be reassuring towards themselves is mediated through memories of parental warmth.[24]

The compassion practice that we used in Jeff's study tries to strengthen a person's parasympathetic system using body posture, breath and a friendly supportive tone of voice. From this position, the person then relates to their setback, disappointment or failure compassionately. What Jeff found using brain-imaging techniques is that when faced with rejection or disappointment, practising compassion helped reduce activation within the amygdala, anterior cingulate and the anterior insula, which are brain regions associated with threat and pain. In contrast, people who were critical of themselves had heightened activation within these neural networks.[25]

But compassion impacts more than the brain; it also impacts our body, and this is where heart rate variability comes in. Overall, we found the compassionate training exercise increased individuals' heart rate variability, but it was more nuanced than this. People who began the trial with lower resting heart rate variability also engaged more with the exercise; that is, they listened to the track more often than those who already had high resting heart rate variability. And they received more self-reported and physiological benefits from the compassion practice. The take-home message is that cultivating compassion results in an increased parasympathetic response, which is very good – having low heart rate variability or low parasympathetic activation is not ideal for physical or mental health.

Why is it that many of us experience an inner voice that tends to be more critical than compassionate? Evolutionary psychiatrist Dr John Price referred to this inner voice as an 'internal referee'. Price was interested in the functions of our emotions, traits and behaviours. He did a lot of work examining defensive behaviours in animals, but also submissive, entrapped and defeat states in humans. One thing he was interested in is how animals know when to attack or submit. How does the animal know they are bigger, faster, stronger or smaller, slower, weaker? Based on our best guesses, animals don't have the same kind of meta-awareness and mental foresight as humans.[26] But something informs them of the state of play – and that is why Price suggested these animals have some kind of subconscious internal referee letting them know to attack or submit.

We humans also have this internal referee, and it narrates our decisions, letting us know if we should challenge someone or be more submissive, or if we have made a mistake or had a success. When we have made a mistake our internal referee can be critical, or even hostile. According to Price, the internal referee often aims to make you behave like you are a subordinate, so you don't challenge a superior. It might say something like 'You have lost; behave like a loser'. In that way, the superior in this situation, perhaps your boss, doesn't see you as threatening and as a result you aren't attacked.

Many of us won't be conscious of these internal dynamics, but we commonly hear statements in therapy like 'I'm just a failure'. This kind of internal referee encourages submissive and passive rather than goal-directed or explorative behaviour, all to reduce potential attacks from superiors.

In one of the most viewed TED Talks of all time, the late Sir Ken Robinson discusses how kids are always happy to take a chance because they aren't frightened of being wrong.[27] He goes on to say that in organisations and businesses today we stigmatise mistakes. Making a mistake is the worst thing we can do. We have internal referees telling us: 'Don't make a mistake; you'll look like a fool. You'll get fired, lose your job, lose status and friendships.' These are great costs. Too great, in fact. So we restrict our creativity and exploration. We play 'better safe than sorry' constantly.

This is what Jeff found by chance in his study, when he was asked how to be self-compassionate. People have well-developed critical internal referees, but the idea of a compassionate internal referee was so novel they needed an explanation of how it might work.

In therapy, I ask clients not only what they say to themselves when they experience a setback or disappointment, but also what the tone of their self-talk is. Is it aggressive, matter-of-fact or blunt? Could it be friendlier? Even compassionate? This relates to how Paul Gilbert founded Compassion Focused Therapy back in the 1980s. He had a client who was extremely self-critical and wasn't responding that well to therapy. So Paul had the genius idea to ask the client to say the words aloud in the same tone as they heard them in their head. To his surprise, when the client said them aloud, she said them in a really angry and contemptuous voice. Researchers have examined this and found when it comes to criticism it is the emotional tone that does more damage than the words.[28] The aim for Paul then was to work with the emotional tone of his client's self-relating, trying to make it more compassionate.

If you speak to yourself like a friend would, trying to be kind and helpful, the same areas of the brain light up as if a friend were actually speaking to you that way.[29] I work with a lot of people who feel they are unlovable and undeserving of kindness or compassion. They are often very good at being kind to others, but the idea of being kind to themselves is completely foreign. They find it threatening. I remember working with one young man who was 26 years old and had difficulties with alcohol and obsessive-compulsive disorder. He was relentlessly self-blaming and self-loathing. So I asked him to close his eyes and say after me, 'May I be safe. May I be free from suffering.' At which point he interrupted me and said, 'I'm not doing this. You don't know the things I've done. I don't want this.' We sat in silence for essentially the rest of the session. He was wiping tears from his face. And he never came back to therapy.

I didn't read the room well at all in that moment. Although I knew he needed compassion, I hadn't explored with him how he felt about it. I made a decision about what would be helpful for him, as opposed to working on that with him.

Almost all of us can resonate with the feeling of having an inner voice monitoring how we are performing. In therapy, we try to become more familiar with the nature of this inner voice, exploring what it sounds like, what it says and its origins.

Sometimes it can be the way a patient's father or teacher spoke to them, which can mean the voice has been there for years, even decades. A lot of people don't recognise that the tone of their inner voice can impact their physiology, much like if it was coming from someone else. This is really important because if somebody was talking to you in angry tones, saying things like 'You're an idiot for doing that', it would make you feel pretty terrible. When we slow things down in therapy and listen to this inner voice, it is common to find that it is self-critical and makes the patient feel pretty terrible. In fact, Paul has noticed that many people criticise themselves before others have the chance, and often more harshly too. That way the criticism doesn't sting as much when it comes from others.

Despite this doom and gloom, there is some hope. Because when people talk to us with caring and compassionate tones, saying things like 'That's really hard to do. It's awesome you gave it a go', it makes us feel safe and connected. We can harness this and create an inner voice that is compassionate. This is what we try to do in therapy.

When we ask people to bring to mind memories of being self-compassionate in Compassion Focused Therapy, they really struggle. I did this exercise far too early in a group program a few years ago, and the patients in the group became very emotional during the exercise, saying things like 'I can't think of a time when I have been'. Now I start by asking patients to bring to mind moments they have been compassionate to others. That works well, as they have lots of examples, and it allows the person to recognise that they are compassionate.

They have got the skills, but they perhaps just haven't directed those skills towards themselves yet.

It is nobody's fault that we find self-compassion difficult. Our brains are designed in such a way that bad seems to be more powerful than good.[30] This is sometimes referred to as 'negativity bias'. This is basically the concept that even when things are equally intense, our brains will notice the bad more than the good. This goes for negative things in both our environment and in our minds. There are some exceptions to this, though. Babies, for example, prefer the positive.[31]

In philosophy there is a powerful thought experiment: 'Imagine the worst day you have ever had in your life, and now imagine your best day. If you had the chance to relive the best day of your life, with the cost of reliving your worst day, would you do it?' Most people say no. The reason is that the worst day was much more painful than the best day was good.[32]

Many evolutionary psychologists have pointed out that we aren't designed to be happy in life, but to survive. As such, our default setting is threat aversion, and thus threatening things hijack our attention more frequently than good things do. It all goes back to the 'better safe than sorry' principle – that smoke detector. By default, our minds are much more likely to go back to negative things and ruminate on them than positive things. One of the core features of depression is when a person gets stuck in this negative ruminative state.

In these situations it is important to remember self-compassion is not just simply soothing badness away. Compassion has an energy to it, and we need energy to help others and ourselves.

When depressed, one thing we lack is energy. In some cases, patients will say they know the reason for their depression and it's because they've never had the energy or confidence to express how they really feel or what they really want. Rather, they are constantly supressing their own needs and wants, and putting everyone else first. In these instances, sometimes what can be most important is to help a patient develop assertiveness. To stop saying yes to everyone's requests despite being burnt out. To put up boundaries. To communicate how they are feeling, be it happy or sad.

I had one patient, Adam, who was in his late 30s and single, and he was quite scared of communicating how he was feeling, because he believed if he did people wouldn't like him. He thought they would see him as difficult and a burden. He told me he was never that popular at school or university, and his colleagues were also his best friends outside of work. Therefore, to say no to some of their requests at work would be a real risk, because he believed it would negatively impact his relationships with them outside of work. At the same time, however, Adam felt stuck at work. He wasn't progressing with his client load, yet he was working overtime constantly, and a lot of that was due to saying yes to helping others out. He also did everything for his family when they needed anything. He always said yes, despite how exhausted or busy he was. So being assertive was something we worked on together, practising in session what Adam could say to respect his boundaries and workload. We would role play it together. Sometimes I would play the role of Adam, while Adam played the role of a colleague or a family member, and other times Adam would play himself and I would be the colleague or family member.

In one of these role plays, I played the role of a colleague and asked Adam if he would help me with some additional paperwork that I had fallen behind on. Adam said, 'Jim, that doesn't sound great. I'd love to help, but I am behind myself. Sorry, I can't.' There was a long pause, and then, 'But I'll be able to help out early tomorrow morning.'

When we reflected on this experience Adam was in tears. Even in a role play he couldn't say no. I asked him what he was so afraid of. His response was that he was scared of being rejected. He deeply believed that by saying no he would be excluded from future events and experience. There was also a part of Adam that liked being asked to do things, because it made him feel needed. And if he started saying no, he wouldn't be needed. 'Who would need me?' he said.

I asked, 'What do you think was going through my mind when you said that you couldn't help?' Adam replied, 'You probably thought I wasn't a team player and you were pissed off with me.' He was projecting his fears onto me, something we commonly do. The most compassionate thing we could do was to help build his assertiveness because that would ease his suffering, but being assertive was a real fear for Adam.

We persisted with role playing and, about six weeks later, Adam came to therapy with a smile. He had said no. He said it was for something minor: a colleague had texted him to see if he could go in to the office on the weekend and help box some equipment that was going to be transported later in the week.

At the time of receiving the text, Adam was just about to go for a run along the beach. He had driven about 45 minutes just to get there. So Adam replied to his colleague saying he couldn't. After sending that text message, Adam said he felt an amazing surge of positive energy. He went on the run. But then the fear kicked in. He started thinking he'd get a text from his boss saying to get to the office and help. Despite checking his messages constantly, nothing ever came.

A few days later in a staff meeting, Adam shared that he would like to take on a new client. The response was an immediate yes, with his supervisor saying she would set it up for him.

When reflecting on these two experiences, Adam said, 'I know it sounds small and trivial, but these two things have given me such a boost. Why didn't I do this sooner?' By being assertive, saying no and sharing his feelings, Adam had unleashed a part of himself he usually tried to suppress. He then said, 'What I'd really like to work on in therapy now is how to start thinking about asking a girl out.' In building assertiveness, he went from never saying no to colleagues to asking to take on a client in a staff meeting and wanting to start dating.

Along this journey, Adam was often self-critical about his efforts. A core component of this work was to ensure in times of trying and having a go he was using a friendly and encouraging inner tone to help him stay committed to what he needed. Other times, when Adam didn't 'succeed' with saying no, he would turn to his ideal compassionate other – which he reported helped soften the blow. Adam also said that just knowing he had this inner ideal compassionate other made him less scared of having a go, because he knew he had the skills to reduce the sense of rejection and loneliness he would feel if it didn't go right. He would say, 'Bruce (the name he gave his ideal compassionate other) has got my back.'

Often as people start the journey towards developing greater self-compassion roadblocks appear. One of these might be the environment in which they work or live. Unfortunately, many people work in organisational settings that are toxic. Maybe the work is demanding, colleagues are critical towards each other or superiors are unsupportive. In some examples, workers in conditions like these are given mindfulness and self-compassion programs to make things better, but this totally neglects the systemic changes needed to make the workplace healthier. It also implies the problem is not the workplace structure or culture, but the individual. It suggests that if you just had greater resilience, mindfulness or self-compassion you would be able to cope with the demands.

The same is true of family settings. I have had patients talk about awful things that have happened to them at the hands of their partners. Australia has a terrible domestic violence problem. In many of these instances, the patient is looking at ways they can better cope. However, often the best thing they can do, the most compassionate thing, is to leave that workplace or family home. We as a society need to provide safe housing, welfare and other supports to help people through these painful experiences.

I sometimes in therapy have patients referred to me who are depressed and also homeless. In these instances I do not guide the patient through a self-compassion exercise, despite the fact that it might be slightly helpful. Rather, I get on the phone and try to find housing and shelter for them. That is what the person needs.

Self-compassion can be a powerful way to relate to yourself, to encourage yourself, to motivate yourself. It doesn't make life easy, but it can make life easier. We are all scared to take risks, make mistakes and be rejected. We can't stop these things from happening, and being self-compassionate doesn't stop them either. It won't inoculate us from pain and suffering. But wouldn't life be much more enjoyable if we weren't so scared of failure? Self-compassion can help give us the courage to take a chance, knowing that if we do fail we can be supportive and reassuring towards ourselves to help ease our own suffering.

8

The anatomy of suffering

Compassion only exists because of suffering, so to fully appreciate what compassion is we must understand what suffering is. I suspect everyone reading this book has at least one powerful story of a time they suffered. But what did that suffering entail? Was it physical or emotional? Was it acute or chronic? Was it social or private? Was it your direct experience or that of someone you cared for? How do we determine what suffering is? Many parents try to minimise the amount of suffering their children experience – just as Buddha's father did.

Buddha's father tried to keep his son, the Indian Prince Siddhartha, in a golden bubble inside the palace walls. He was trying to protect his son from all the suffering of life because of how much he loved him. A misguided way of showing his love, perhaps, but nevertheless understandable. Siddhartha remained in that golden palace for 29 years, eventually escaping with the help of one of his assistants. The story goes that outside, Siddhartha was shocked with what he saw, as he encountered disease, ageing and death for the first time. This would have sent most of us back to the palace, but Siddhartha was so shocked by the suffering, aware it was his destiny too, that he became preoccupied with finding a solution for the human condition.[1] Siddhartha never returned to the palace, leaving behind his wife, son and father, as he was determined to fully understand suffering. His father's strategy of keeping his son protected from the realities of the world had backfired spectacularly.

On his quest, Siddhartha encountered many philosophies, insights and contemplative practices to address suffering, eventually arriving at the famous Bodhi Tree. For many days, he sat quietly observing the rising and falling of his own mental phenomena. From this experience he became aware that our minds can be filled with conflicting and difficult motives and passions – ones of not-wanting (aversions) and of wanting (grasping after what is impermanent). Through observing his mind, he recognised how easily we can be absorbed and taken by whatever desires and passions happen to be stimulated within us.[2]

Siddhartha's solution to this was twofold. First, train the mind to become aware of thoughts as they arise, so that we can become mindful rather than mindless in our emotions and actions. Second, study all the passions and desires in us and focus on those that can offset grasping, greed and aversion, to balance the mind and bring true calmness in working towards compassion – the desire to see all beings free of suffering. In this way the mind can be given a focus. Mindfulness brings stability to the mind and compassion transforms it, freeing us from egoistic pursuits.[3]

This is a very condensed version of a remarkable life that gave rise to Buddhism, which has had a significant impact on how we understand and study compassion. But of course, compassion and suffering are not owned by Buddhism. All the major religions have compassion as a core pillar in their teachings.

Not all suffering is equal, and I use the term 'suffering' to encompass all sorts of tragedies, from emotional to physical, low level to extreme. It is clear that being upset is not equivalent to the suffering encountered from atrocities like war, rape and torture. There is also a distinction between chosen suffering and that which is thrust upon you. Chosen suffering could be the mental anguish I experience as I try to write this book. Sometimes this is better captured by the term 'effort'. It isn't pleasant and I'm often frustrated, but this struggle to write comes with meaning and hopefully a positive outcome. As they say, we suffer for our art. Unchosen suffering – like being assaulted, losing your child to cancer, being born into a war-torn region – is very different. We wouldn't choose to experience this kind of suffering.

So what is suffering? There is a term in Buddhism, *dukkha*, that in its simplest form means 'unsatisfactory'. We are often in unsatisfactory states, craving certain things and not getting them, and this turmoil gives rise to suffering. The Oxford Lexico dictionary defines suffering as 'the state of undergoing pain, distress, or hardship'. Many of us use suffering as a synonym for pain and distress. And this is how mindfulness came to be so popular in the West, to help with pain.

Jon Kabat-Zinn introduced this concept to many with the program he developed called 'Mindfulness-Based Stress Reduction' (MBSR). The premise here is those with chronic pain suffer deeply and, although we are unable to remove their pain, we can help with the subjective experience of pain. The program was originally eight weeks long, with two-hour sessions, but it has been used in various formats since (shorter, longer and online). MBSR has been evaluated dozens of times and meta-analytic evidence shows it is helpful at not only reducing subjective pain for those with chronic health conditions, but also improving their quality of life and wellbeing.[4]

How we address suffering in helpful ways is at the core of all caring professions. In Buddhism, one approach is to practise the four immeasurables (friendly-kindness, equanimity, appreciative joy and compassion). But not all people wish to pursue Buddhism to address their suffering. This is where the work of Kabat-Zinn is so influential. In his seminal book, *The Full Catastrophe of Living*, Kabat-Zinn outlines how he hoped to bring mindfulness and the benefits it can afford to people in the West who struggle with the suffering they experience, specifically chronic pain. But he wanted to do this without reference to Buddhism, as he feared that it might be seen as too New Age or 'mystic'. So he developed the secular MBSR program, which is now used throughout the world.

To address suffering mindfully, a key aim is to bring yourself into contact with the concept of impermanence. That is, the nature of life is such that things only last for a small period of time. Nothing remains the same. Everything changes. As Alice Morse Earle famously said, 'Yesterday is history. Tomorrow is a mystery. Today is a gift. That's why it is called the present.' Building from this concept, mindfulness can then shape the way we experience things, including how we experience suffering. This approach underpins the MBSR program. Kabat-Zinn defines mindfulness as 'paying attention to the present moment, on purpose, and non-judgementally'.

As discussed earlier, mindfulness can be as simple (*and* as complicated) as focusing your attention on the rising and falling of your breath. Many find a great sense of calm from anchoring their attention in this way, but for others this can be a frustrating process. When you try it for the first time you quickly become aware that your attention jumps around a lot. People get frustrated for a whole range of reasons, but two of the most common are not being able to do the practice 'right' and not being able to empty their mind of thoughts and emotions. It is ironic that the very thing aimed to help with suffering, mindfulness practice, can be the cause of further suffering, as we grasp for a life without pain, without suffering. But this is not what mindfulness is about.

The aim of mindfulness is not to bring you to a relaxed state, though this can be a by-product of focusing on the breath. The aim of mindfulness is to bring your attention to the present moment, which means being open to any state you might be in, whether that is pleasant or unpleasant. As Kabat-Zinn points out, the aim is to be with whatever state with an attitude of non-judgement.

But what does non-judgement mean? From a Compassion Focused Therapy perspective, we would say it means to be with what is and not attack or criticise it. Sometimes that means being curious and having an attitude of friendliness towards your inner experiences, but this can take time to develop. The ripple effect of this is your relationship to these experiences – emotional, cognitive, sensory – can change, as you shift from fighting them or being hooked in them, to curiously observing them, then letting the experiences pass as your focus remains on the breath. Again, this is much easier said than done.

Other mindfulness practices can involve repeating a mantra, the most famous probably being 'Om', which is believed by some to be the first sound that originated on Earth.[5]

Regardless of what your focus is on, mindfulness is not about emptying your mind, that's not possible, but rather about bringing a greater awareness to your whole-body experience. It opens your attention, which allows you to experience suffering in a slightly different way.

To act compassionately means noticing and attending to suffering. Do you notice your own suffering or the suffering around you? Or are you so focused on your daily tasks, which are often immense, that you miss, minimise or deny the suffering you experience? For example, as I write this I am trying to ignore the pain in my neck and lower back. I know if I do some brief stretches prescribed by my physiotherapist the pain will subside, yet I keep writing, putting off this helpful self-care strategy. Many of us are guilty of this. Usually I will wait until I can no longer ignore the pain and then I have to get up.

Mindfulness, therefore, is a really helpful way to become aware of our own suffering and the suffering around us. The best way to learn about mindfulness is to experience it. There are many books on mindfulness, as well as many mindfulness-based apps you can access, with increasing evidence showing these apps can also be helpful.[6]

Just a cautionary note: despite what you can read on blogs, mindfulness isn't some kind of panacea or life hack that leads to miracles for all. It can take quite some time to get a feel for it, taking many small steps along the way. If you are new to mindfulness, it can be very helpful to have guided support. If you just throw yourself at it and enrol in a ten-day Vipassana retreat, it can be a very difficult experience, like running a marathon without doing any prior training. It is important to take your time with the practice, slowly getting more comfortable with it and your inner psyche. Some people don't respond well to mindfulness. They will find it difficult no matter how much they practise. For some, it can make them more anxious, or even increase feelings of pain and headaches. But for most the responses are positive.[7]

Mindfulness is one way of helping us bring our attention back to our intentions of compassion. Intentions are what our minds tend to circle back to, as we remember the things we need to do. For example, we may intend to buy milk on the way home. Wanting to remember this increases the chances we will.[8] We can leverage that for compassion. If we intend to be compassionate, we will circle back to it, looking for ways to enact it. But sometimes we need help, as we can get caught up in the busyness of everyday life, or the heat of the moment in an argument. Mindfulness can help with this.

I had one patient who found he always got angry when driving, often swearing or tailgating other drivers. He said, 'It's terrible. I know I shouldn't do it, but when someone cuts me off, I don't know how to stop yelling and swearing. It's like I have to give them back some of their own medicine.' Road rage is a real problem, and many of us have experienced it in some form or another. My patient wanted to address his road rage, because he had children and he didn't want them to see him react so badly. In one therapy session he said, 'My daughter once said to me, "Dad, I don't want to get in the car with you. You'll just get angry. What if you start swearing or yelling at one of my teachers?"' It was at that point my patient knew he needed to do something.

What my patient's story captures is how often we can get caught up in the emotion of something and say or do something we don't really mean. In other words, mentally we are no longer in the driver's seat, as the anger and rage is deciding our actions for us. Mindfulness can help with this process. It can give us that little bit of breathing room to respond to our situations in ways that are helpful or congruent with our values and morals, as opposed to simply reacting and being on autopilot.

Mindfulness can be a powerful way of short-circuiting our tendency to punish and cause further suffering.

Many of us harbour beliefs that some deserve to suffer. In some parts of the US and other countries (Iran, Saudi Arabia, North Korea), the death penalty still exists as a form of punishment. Some compassion theorists suggest there are two forms of compassion: one is for those who suffer even though they have done nothing wrong (e.g., a victim) and one is for those who suffer because they did something wrong (e.g., someone in jail for a crime). Absolute compassion applies to both, whereas relative compassion addresses the difference between the former and the latter. This is an interesting dimension to compassion and suffering.

Many of us believe that when we do something bad we should be punished, much like Eve was when she ate the forbidden apple. But what is the function of punishing ourselves? One hypothesis that an Australian team of researchers tested is whether punishment reduces feelings of guilt associated with an immoral deed. The study by Dr Brock Bastian and his colleagues was cleverly called 'Cleansing the Soul by Hurting the Flesh'.[9] In the study, they asked participants to either write about a time they did something immoral – for example, when they rejected or socially excluded someone – or write about a recent everyday social interaction. Afterwards they asked the same participants to submerge their non-dominant hand into an ice bucket and keep it there for as long as they could.

What they found is participants who wrote about the immoral behaviour held their hands in for longer and rated it as more painful than those who wrote about an everyday interaction. Critically, they also found that this physical suffering made them feel less guilty about the immoral deed. It seems, to some degree at least, that the punishment served a purpose; it ironically helped reduce some of the suffering they had around the immoral act.

I was reminded of this study when listening to a patient of mine talking about punishing himself for an immoral act he committed. He was with his girlfriend for at least ten years, and during this time they both had one affair, both purely sexual. Both forgave each other and continued with the relationship. But then he had another affair, which was more than sex this time. He had feelings for this other person. He told his girlfriend, and she broke up with him. Despite this, they remained good friends and regularly caught up, and still had sex together. He wanted to kickstart the relationship again, but she did not.

This patient came to therapy for help because he'd been devastated since the official break-up. He felt numb and said he couldn't believe how stupid he had been. He had stopped doing things he enjoyed, constantly ruminating over his 'idiocy' and criticising himself. Meanwhile, his ex-girlfriend seemed relatively happy. She had forgiven him, but nevertheless did not want to date him again. I asked him, 'How long do you need to continue to punish yourself for this?' He said, 'I don't know.'

After a couple of sessions, it became clear that he had to punish himself to show her how bad he felt. If he stopped doing this, he believed it would look to her as if he was letting himself off the hook, or that he didn't really care about her. Because, ultimately, he wanted to get back together with her. He said he would only stop punishing himself when they were back together. He believed that if he stopped before then, there was no chance of getting back together. So the punishment had a purpose. Indeed, he believed not getting back together was more painful than the punishment he was inflicting.

This is where self-compassion could be so helpful, but for many, like my patient, there is a deep fear that being self-compassionate means letting themselves off the hook. People can fear this in instances of moral transgression, believing it can increase the likelihood they will transgress again. How wrong this thinking is.

Drs Juliana Breines and Serena Chen found that self-compassion predicted making amends and avoiding repeating moral transgressions.[10] In Breines and Chen's study, participants were asked to recall a time when they did something wrong that they felt bad about – for example, cheating on a significant other – and write about it. Participants were then assigned to a self-compassion condition, a self-esteem condition or a positive-distraction control condition. In the self-compassion condition participants were told to reflect on the event and write a paragraph to themselves from a compassionate perspective, expressing kindness and understanding. In the self-esteem condition they were instructed to write about their positive qualities, for example, personal attributes and accomplishments they were proud of. And in the positive-distraction control condition participants wrote about a hobby they enjoyed. After this the researchers asked participants about their desire to make amends and their commitment to not repeat the transgression in the future. Those in the self-compassion condition were significantly more motivated to make amends and avoid repeating the transgression compared to those in the self-esteem or positive-distraction conditions.

It seems humans like to suffer; we like to punish ourselves. One clever study put participants in a lab room in which they could push a button and shock themselves if they wanted to. But they could also just sit there and do nothing; be with their thoughts or even meditate if they wanted. The participants were left in the room for 15 minutes. What happened? Well, 67% of men and 25% of women chose to shock themselves rather than just sit quietly and think. What is amazing with this study is that, prior to it, participants had stated they would pay money to avoid being shocked.[11]

I took my son tenpin bowling recently, and at the venue were several arcade games. One arcade game was a big 'electric chair' you could sit in and pay to get an electric shock. As you might have guessed, there was a huge line of people waiting for that game. Paul Bloom unpacks some of the paradoxical pleasures we can get from this kind of chosen suffering in his book *The Sweet Spot*.

Although compassion is focused on alleviating and preventing suffering, this does not mean being compassionate involves avoiding all hardship and suffering. That was Siddhartha's father's error. We tend to value things more when we have had to work for them, and we can learn the values of patience, persistence and understanding through suffering.[12] Some researchers have also found that those who have experienced a level of adversity are more compassionate to others.[13] You will sometimes hear in compassion meditations the mantra 'May I be free from suffering'. That does not mean free from effort, hard work, disease, ageing and dying. Rather it means: may I be free from my natural and completely understandable aversions to this reality. Often, our want to fight against or resist these realities is what causes greater suffering.

In therapy we come into contact with the parts of our lives that cause us suffering, which is very difficult. Our natural instinct is to try not to think about the pain we hold, escaping or avoiding it. Moving towards this pain is the last thing we want to do. But moving towards suffering is not purposeless in this case. It's not easy. But it can make things easier.

In Buddhism there is the *sutra* of the two arrows. The first arrow creates pain, while the second arrow is the suffering that arises from our reactions to the first. In Compassion Focused Therapy we suggest there is also a third arrow, which is when we feel ashamed of our reactions and fight or try to suppress them. So *dukkha* relates not to the pain itself, but our reactions, our fear and rage about experiencing pain. When Kabat-Zinn pioneered the introduction of mindfulness for chronic pain for which medicine could do little, the aim was to work with the emotional reactions to pain (the second arrow) rather than the pain itself (the first arrow).

When we talk about pain as a synonym of suffering in medical terms, often the aim is to remove it, which makes sense. It many ways modern medicine – which is an absolute gift and so important for us all – is mostly interested in the first arrow. We have scientists all over the world dedicating their lives to reducing and removing our pain, with thousands of success stories and miracles. Professor Tom Sensky made the observation that we experience pain in particular parts of our body, which doctors try to heal, but suffering is to do with the whole person.[14] When we have a broken leg we say, 'I have pain in my leg'; we don't say, 'My leg is suffering'. Suffering is concerned with our whole experience and as a result with our second arrow experience of pain.

When we view pain as something to get rid of, it narrows our focus on the pain itself, and we don't consider the pain as something we might grow through or learn from. Heartbreak is an example of this kind of pain. It's not pleasant, but with time we can begin to understand and relate to it differently. There are thousands of songs, books, poems and films that depict this experience. The entire rom-com genre of Hollywood plays on it. When we have experienced heartbreak, we connect with these stories on a deeper level.

There has been recent work examining a phenomenon called 'post-traumatic growth', which describes a positive psychological change that is experienced as a result of a highly challenging and stressful circumstance. The book *Choose Growth*, by Drs Scott Barry Kaufman and Jordyn Feingold, takes a deep dive into what is meant by growth and provides suggestions on how to go about pursuing meaning after experiencing painful difficulties and challenges.[15] As Kaufman and Feingold point out, just choosing to 'grow' after experiencing a challenging and painful experience

148

doesn't work like flicking a light switch. It is often difficult and takes time and support, with many oscillating between striving for change and avoiding it, because the pain is so difficult.

Australian clinical psychologist Dr David Roland wrote the book *The Power of Suffering*, which describes people's personal encounters with suffering, such as domestic violence, bullying or the sudden loss of a loved one, and how these painful experiences over time shaped them and led them to do things with their lives that brought them great meaning.[16] This phenomenon of course does not transpire for all of us. And a life without these tragedies would be preferred, as we can still have a life of great meaning without tragedy. However, it does shed light on the powerful things we discover about ourselves when we go through painful suffering. Christina Feldman and Professor Willem Kuyken suggest that compassion recognises that not all pain can be fixed or cured, but suffering is made more approachable in a landscape of compassion.[17]

When deciding to act compassionately, the level of suffering can be too much for us, and we have to turn away. This is sometimes referred to as personal distress. For example, many people find blood distressing, closing their eyes or turning away from it. Other people can find sadness too difficult to tolerate and walk away when others cry. But another important dimension to suffering is that sometimes to help others we need to make a sacrifice, and these sacrifices can stop us from acting compassionately.

To examine this phenomenon, I ran a series of studies with my PhD student Mitchell Green and developmental psychologist

Professor Mark Nielsen to examine the compassionate responses of four-year-old children. In these experiments a child and a puppet (controlled by an experimenter) needed to complete the same task independently, and they were both informed that if they successfully completed the task they would win a sticker. Four-year-old children interact with puppets as if they are their own agents, and they love winning stickers, so they were really motivated to complete the task. In the experiment the puppets never had enough resources to complete the task. And we wanted to see how children reacted to that. Would they help the puppet or not?

To make matters interesting, we made the experiment such that children would have either ample resources or just enough resources to complete the tasks themselves – this was the cost condition, because if the child helped the puppet it would mean giving them one of their own pieces and thus they would have sacrificed their chance at winning the sticker. In a final manipulation, when the puppet realised it couldn't complete the task it would either not be bothered by it or start crying – the suffering condition.

What we found is when the child had ample resources they helped the puppet all the time. They would take their extra pieces and help the puppet complete the task almost immediately, even before the puppet realised it couldn't complete the task. However, when the child only had enough pieces to complete the task themselves, they never helped the puppet. Even when the puppet started crying and was upset, the child still wouldn't help the puppet. We gave each child and puppet three tasks to do, and across all three tasks the child never helped the puppet if there was a cost to helping.[18]

We have completed several variations of this experiment with over 240 children: one where the child completes the tasks with an adult instead of a puppet, one where we take away the chance of winning any stickers, and another where we make the puppet an in-group member. None of these variations has led to children helping the target (be it puppet or adult) when there is a cost to helping. The sacrifice of not winning is too large. The only exception to this is when we remove the rewards and explicitly instruct the child that they can share and demonstrate how to do so. In this condition we found significantly more children helped the puppet.[19] This doesn't mean children are selfish or bad. It isn't the child's fault for not helping. Rather the study shows that when there is a cost to helping others, the likelihood of us responding helpfully is reduced, even when the target is distressed and crying.

What is encouraging, however, is that although the children didn't actively help the puppet by sharing their pieces in the cost condition, they did offer passive forms of compassion. They would say things like 'It's okay' and 'Maybe next time', or stroke the puppet to make it feel better. Some children even asked the experimenter if they had any more pieces, while others searched the room for more pieces. These actions suggest children do want to help, they just don't want to if it means they can't win their sticker.

To reiterate the earlier point I made, not all suffering is equal. In these experiments with children and puppets the suffering is extremely low. The level of suffering experienced in situations such as cancer, rape or torture is not the same; it is in a different stratosphere altogether.

Sacrifice is an interesting concept to consider with suffering, though. What are we willing to sacrifice to help another who is suffering? Is it time, money, resources? Many of us happily sacrifice our hard-earned money by donating it to charity or voting for higher taxes, so that others who need it can benefit. Would you be willing to sacrifice one of your cars or one of your extra properties so that someone else could have a chance at a better life? Are you willing to live with less? Would you sacrifice one of your organs, say a kidney, to someone who needed it?

Dr Abigail Marsh and her team studies what she calls 'extreme altruists'. These are people who do extraordinary acts that require sacrifice, such as donating a kidney to a complete stranger. She explores the reasoning behind these extraordinarily altruistic acts with interviews, brain imaging, behavioural games and self-report measures. She's found that what underpins this extreme altruism is social discounting. Social discounting means we tend to value those who are closer to us, both relationally (family member vs stranger) and in proximity (neighbour vs someone living 500 kilometres away), more than those further away.[20] This harks back to Peter Singer's drowning child thought experiment. Extreme altruists are seemingly inoculated against social discounting, and value strangers just as much as family and friends.

But how do we help people reduce their tendency to socially discount and adopt a more morally expansive mindset, one where they are concerned for the welfare of others beyond their typical boundaries? New work by Charlie Crimston, Dr April Hoang and myself have found that with Compassionate Mind Training we can significantly increase people's moral concern, so that it includes those typically beyond it, such as out-groups, stigmatised groups, animals, plants and even the environment.[21] However, I am unsure if the intervention is powerful enough to lead to extraordinary acts of altruism, such as donating kidneys to strangers. That is an idea for future research.

Unfortunately, many of us in positions of power struggle with the idea of giving away our resources, and we have seen this to some degree with the rollout of COVID-19 vaccines across the world, with rich and developed countries securing millions of doses, but vulnerable and poorer countries having little access. How do we remedy these disparities? I do not know.

Looking to the positive, during the COVID-19 years it has been extraordinary to see how many people have volunteered and raced out of retirement to help, at great cost to themselves. All with the motivation to save lives and prevent suffering. Through the lockdowns we have seen towns and communities come together in solidarity to try to minimise the levels of suffering in the community.

We suffer every day. We make sacrifices every day. Life is made more bearable by the fact so many of us approach these difficulties with compassion.

9

When compassion collapses

On 2 September 2015, three-year-old boy Alan Kurdi appeared across our televisions and newspapers when his small lifeless body washed ashore on a Turkish beach. Alan drowned in the Mediterranean Sea when his family were trying to escape Syria, seeking refuge in Greece. A picture of Alan went viral on social media (more than 20 million people viewed it) with the hashtag #KiyiyaVuranInsanlik, translated as 'humanity washed ashore'.[1] Alan's death seized global attention. It brought a face to the civil war and refugee crisis that had been unfolding for years in Syria, which the global community had done their best to ignore.

The image of Alan's body had an immediate impact, with a dramatic increase in global search terms related to the Syrian crisis, and Red Cross donations increasing a hundredfold. Not surprisingly, however, those donations returned to baseline only five weeks later.[2] One encouraging finding was that the number of donors who signed up for repeated monthly contributions increased by a factor of ten during that period, from 106 to 1061 donors. Sweden even accepted 150,000 Syrian refugees, which is a remarkably high number given its population in 2015 was just under 10 million.[3]

Another remarkable compassionate response came from Angela Merkel, then chancellor of Germany, who accepted over a million refugees. Merkel said, in response to the growing refugee tragedy, 'Germany is a strong country ... we have managed so many things – we can do this.' The phrase *'wir schaffen das'*, or 'we can do this', cut through, but not always in the way she had hoped. She was criticised both domestically and internationally. However, she stayed committed, saying, 'If we start having to apologise for showing a friendly face in an emergency situation, then this is not my country.' Compassionate responding like this takes courage.

When we are confronted with images of suffering like Alan's, we are spurred into action. If only we had acted sooner, then perhaps Alan would still be here today, growing older and pursuing his dreams. Prior to Alan's image being front-page news, about 250,000 people (including children) had died during the Syrian war, yet the world was eerily quiet on this unfolding tragedy. Is this a surprise? The quote 'One person's death is a tragedy; a million deaths is a statistic' is often attributed to Josef Stalin and, sadly, it seems this couldn't be truer. It is hard not to be shaken by images of a vulnerable little boy losing his life. According to a report from Save the Children, there are 415 million children living in war-torn countries right now.[4]

When talking to Paul Gilbert about this he said to me,

> It is quite extraordinary that, given what we know about how early lives affect brain maturation and even genetic expression, we have such limited resources dedicated to the desire for every child to grow up in a compassionate environment. This failure to grasp the size and nature of the problem of how children around the world are raised in appalling conditions is probably humanity's greatest compassion failure.[5]

In psychology, Alan's story is an example of 'the identifiable victim effect'. We can empathise and connect with individual people, but when we scale it up to thousands or millions of people, we struggle to comprehend the sheer size of the suffering. We simply can't connect. In fact, the greater the number of people suffering, the more it can feel like we can't make a difference. These types of responses are referred to as 'the arithmetic of compassion', a phenomenon researched by Professor Paul Slovic.

Essentially, the arithmetic of compassion refers to how numbers matter when it comes to compassion, though not in the way we would think. The more people suffering, the less likely it is we will respond with compassion. It is a paradox.

Three of the most dominant and well-researched aspects to this paradox are: the collapse of compassion, compassion fade and psychological numbing. These three theories are very similar but vary slightly. Compassion collapse is our tendency to turn away from mass suffering. Compassion fade is the tendency to experience a decrease in empathy as the number of people in need of help increases. Finally, psychological numbing is our diminished sensitivity to the value of life and our inability to appreciate loss.

All three of these theories can help explain why we were not moved to action for the 250,000 lost lives in Syria, but we were for the one lost life of Alan. Paraphrasing Slovic, we aren't moved by numbers. But the iconic image of Alan's body on the shore of a Turkish beach hit us like a bolt of lightning. Visual imagery gives us an emotional experience, and it is this emotion that motivates us to act. The identifiable victim effect is powerful. But if we see more people suffering, we are less likely to act. There have been countless examples of this across the course of humanity, a recent one being the Rwandan genocide, in which 8000 people were dying a day. The international community largely failed to intervene.

So at what point do the numbers lead to compassion collapse? Is it 100, 100,000 or 1,000,000? This is the question that Slovic with his collaborators tried to understand in a clever experiment.[6] The researchers in this study were specifically examining compassion fade (a decrease in empathy as numbers increase), as opposed to collapse of compassion, but the two are closely entwined. Participants were given the opportunity to donate money to Save the Children. One group of participants were asked to donate money to feed a seven-year-old African girl named Rokia, an identified victim. Another group were asked to donate to feed a nine-year-old boy, Moussa. A third group were asked to donate to both Rokia and Moussa. The experimenters measured how many Swedish crowns (SEK) each participant was willing to donate, and their feelings about donating, as well as whether their donation would make a real difference.

What the experiment found is that participants were willing to donate equally to Rokia and Moussa. That's where the good news ends. When Rokia and Moussa were paired together, the willingness to donate significantly dropped. In addition, the participants' feelings of sympathy towards them significantly dropped. Participants believed their donation would make more of a difference in the single-child conditions than in the paired condition.

The sceptics reading this would point out that the participants just signalled their willingness to give money; they didn't actually give any. And that's a valid point. The experimenters thought similarly, so in a follow-up study with a new group of 168 participants, the participants were asked to complete a range of questionnaires and were given 70 SEK as payment for their effort. These participants were then instructed that they had the opportunity to donate their just-earned 70 SEK to Save the Children. Here the experiment was the same; participants were assigned to either just reading about Rokia, just reading about Moussa, or reading about both. The results? The exact same. Participants donated less, felt less sympathy, and believed the money made less of a difference in the paired condition compared to the single-child conditions. It seems our compassion for others begins to drop when we reach two people.

Slovic and his team have also examined how interventions might affect our behaviour when we're confronted with statistical and identifiable victims. A statistical victim is a victim presented in terms of numbers (250,000 deaths in Syria), whereas an identifiable victim is a specific person with a name and background (Alan Kurdi). In a study with his collaborators Professors Deborah Small and George Loewenstein, Slovic wanted to test two hypotheses: firstly, thinking analytically about the value of lives will lead to reduced giving to an identifiable victim; secondly, analytical thinking will have no effect on giving to statistical victims.[7]

In this study, participants completed surveys for which they received five one-dollar bills. They were then given a receipt, a blank envelope, and a charity request letter. The participants were instructed to read the letter carefully, before signing the receipt and returning the letter in the envelope. The letter started by describing how the participant could donate any of their just earned five dollars to the organisation Save the Children. Specifically, they were told, 'any money donated will go towards relieving the severe food crisis in Southern Africa and Ethiopia'. The rest of the letter for participants assigned to the statistical-victim condition contained factual information from the Save the Children website about the problems of starvation in Africa. Participants assigned to the identifiable-victim condition, on the other hand, received a picture of a little girl and a brief description of her.

But Slovic and his team also had an intervention aspect to this study. This was a brief lesson about identifiability. Before the experiment began, half the participants were told about how research shows people typically react more strongly to specific people with problems, rather than to statistics about people with problems. The participants were even presented with the example of 'Baby Jessica', who fell into a well in Texas in 1989. People sent over $700,000 for her rescue effort, whereas the thousands of children who die in car accidents each year seldom evoke such strong reactions. Would this intervention lead to reduced donations to the statistical victim like the researchers hypothesised, or would it be in the other direction?

What they found didn't surprise the researchers, but it did sadden optimistic me. The intervention didn't lead to more money being donated to the statistical victim, but it did lead to significantly less money being donated to the identifiable victim. The intervention was successful at reducing our compassionate donations to individuals, but it completely failed at improving our compassionate donations to statistical victims.

When we think analytically this reduces our natural tendency to want to give to individuals, but it has no impact on statistical victims. Slovic and his team tried a number of variations on this study, with some experiments using slightly different framing, others presenting identifiable information alongside statistical information, and finally others again inducing a 'feeling' or 'calculated' mode of mind. None of these variations improved donations to the statistical victims, and all led to reduced giving to the identifiable victim. The conclusion is that emotions are a vastly more effective pathway to compassionate action than deliberative thinking.

Another way of looking at this is that deliberative thinking leads to more consistent giving regardless of type of victim. As individuals, we have limited money we can donate (for the most part). Yet we can be easily swept up by our emotions and donate more than is needed to specific charities using identifiable victims. A good recent example of this is when a five-month-old baby was tragically killed when her mother, carrying her, was swooped by a magpie and fell over. The mother's family started a GoFundMe page for the parents that accrued so much money they turned off donations after only 24 hours. But so many people still wanted to donate that they reopened the donations. People were so moved by this story that they wanted to help even when there was no clear indication of what more money could do.

Thinking analytically might mean we are less swept up in our emotions and consequently don't get caught in this predicament of giving more than is needed. Therefore, we might find ourselves in a position where we have more money available to donate to more statistical victims, the idea being to give a little bit of money to many people, as opposed to a lot of money to a few. However, I am unaware of any specific research examining this hypothesis. I am inclined to think that we don't do this, and rather just keep the money for ourselves.

Though in certain contexts I am sure deliberative thinking would lead to more compassionate actions. We just need to do more research to learn more.

Slovic has also examined the concept of psychological numbing, our inability to appreciate losses of life as they become larger. When the numbers are small, they have an impact, but the impact diminishes as the number increases.

There is an easy thought experiment to demonstrate this. Do you feel any different about the loss of life when you consider 15 million dying compared to 75 million? Not so much, right? It was possible to see this effect taking place with COVID-19. The number of deaths were rattled off at press conferences almost with ease, with underlying health conditions often being used to justify the loss. Little time or emotion was committed to feeling the losses; the emphasis tended to be on any new freedoms coming. To try to counteract the psychological numbness caused by COVID-19, and to demonstrate the immensity of the loss, an outdoor art installation in the US comprising 650,000 small white flags was created. Each white flag represents a life lost to COVID-19. When numbers get too large, visual imagery can jolt us back to the devastating reality, to remember that each number represents an individual person.

A striking paradox in the arithmetic of compassion is that people predict they will feel more compassion when many are suffering rather than less. Moral philosophy also speaks to this issue, with consequentialism – most famously, utilitarianism – positing that saving more lives is the morally right thing to do.

Yet, as Slovic's TED Talk title states, 'The More Who Die, the Less We Care'.

Another team of researchers have been studying the phenomenon of collapse of compassion. According to research conducted by Drs Daryl Cameron and Keith Payne, people believe that they will have more intense feelings of compassion for larger numbers, but that this will be both financially and emotionally costly (due to needing to give and feel more). Therefore, when confronted with large numbers of people suffering, individuals strategically turn off their compassion.

We might also turn off our compassion because we believe that if we do help, our contribution won't make that much of a difference. Slovic coined the term 'pseudoinefficacy', which refers to the phenomenon of people being less willing to provide aid to one person once they become aware of the larger numbers of people they are unable to help. Their help will be like a drop in the ocean, they reason, so why bother? Cameron and Payne believe our compassion collapse is not because we aren't emotionally moved by a situation, but rather because of how we end up controlling our emotions. We have a tendency to shut off our sympathy to large groups. In other words, we avoid becoming overwhelmed.

In their seminal study, Cameron and Payne tried to find a way of reversing the collapse of compassion.[8] Participants were presented with a description of either one or eight child refugees from the war-torn region of Darfur in Sudan. Half of the participants were told that later in the experiment they would be asked to donate money towards the victim/s.

The other half were not. According to Cameron and Payne's theory, helping eight victims is more costly (both financially and emotionally) than helping one, so informing participants of an impending donation should turn off compassion for the group of eight. Not telling them would remove the financial incentive to turn off compassion, which Cameron and Payne hoped would reverse compassion collapse.

What did they find? When participants were told they would be asked to donate later, they showed more compassion for the individual than for the eight victims, as expected. But when there was no financial cost, the effect reversed, and more compassion was felt for the eight. Although this result is encouraging, the study did not actually measure donation behaviour.

The other interesting twist that Cameron and Payne studied is the hypothesis that those skilled with emotion regulation would fall prey to the collapse of compassion when cost was imposed. In a series of experiments, participants were always informed that later in the experiment there would be an expectation to donate money towards the victim/s. What the researchers found is those who were not particularly good at regulating emotions did not experience a collapse of compassion when confronted with either one or eight victims. But those who were highly skilled with regulating their emotions did reduce the compassion they felt as the number of victims increased.

In a follow-up to this, the researchers told a new group of participants to allow their emotions to flow freely, whereas another group were told to control their emotions. And, as you might have predicted, those who were told to let their emotions go freely did not restrict their compassion, but those who did control their emotions experienced a collapse of compassion for larger numbers.

These findings match what Slovic and his team of researchers found: when we work with our deliberative pathway and control our emotions, thinking analytically, our tendency to be compassionate drops.

Reading all of this research you would be forgiven for feeling somewhat discouraged. Right now, the world is facing a tsunami of catastrophes: the climate-change crisis, pandemics, ongoing wars in the Middle East as well as new wars in Europe, and the weekly murdering of women in domestic violence. What can we do to help resolve our tendency to be unmoved by large numbers and statistics?

There is no simple answer here, and large-scale coordinated levels of help are needed to support compassionate actions. We can train people individually in compassion, but individual interventions are not enough; we need system-level support. A perfect illustration of this is in nursing.

There is a phenomenon referred to as 'compassion fatigue', which postulates that we can become exhausted from caring too much too often. The term was coined by Professor Charles Figley, who developed a scale to measure this effect. However, research by a number of independent scholars has found that this concept of compassion fatigue is not well understood and poorly defined.[9] When people say 'compassion fatigue' what they really mean is either they have empathised with a person and have not moved on to doing something about it, which has led to personal distress,[10] or they're burnt out, which in the majority of cases is due to not being well enough supported.

The issue of burnout is a constant in most healthcare workplaces, where the expectation to do more with less support and less compassion from management is increasing. In one study, researchers interviewed nurses who were exposed to high levels of suffering.[11] When asked what support they would like to help with their exhaustion, nurses often said that if their wards were properly staffed they could spend more time with each of their patients, which would make their job easier. These types of sentiments suggest that the nurses wanted to spend more time with people suffering, not less, but they weren't adequately supported by management to do their job. This is where burnout stems from.

This couldn't be better exemplified than in the UK, where nurses were only given a 1% pay rise during COVID-19. This was described as 'pitiful' by the Royal College of Nursing. What made this pill particularly difficult to swallow was the fact the government had been saying daily how amazing the nurses had been, the 'unsung heroes', encouraging people to line the streets to applaud them. But when this kind of praise is not backed up with financial support, it makes people feel insulted, unvalued and unrecognised. This is what leads to burnout, and staff leaving the profession.[12]

There is a famous 1891 painting called *The Doctor*, by Luke Fildes. It depicts a doctor in the early hours of the morning sitting attentively by the bed of his patient, a sick child in the final stages of life. The painting portrays the values of the physician; although he cannot help the patient escape the unavoidable, he is compassionately present. It is supposedly an image inspired by the painter's own personal experience of the loss of his son.

In a recent book called *Compassionomics*, Drs Stephen Trzeciak and Anthony Mazzarelli discuss the powerful impact this painting has, depicting the important doctor–patient relationship.[13] Trzeciak and Mazzarelli have done compelling research documenting the crucial role that compassion has in improving the medical care we provide patients.

Recently, Trzeciak asked a child who was receiving regular care to draw the doctor's clinic. In the drawing the child is surrounded by his family as he sits on a hospital bed, with the doctor at his computer screen. This drawing is eye-opening. It appears the environments in which we provide medical care have shifted markedly, and for the doctor the computer requires greater attention than the patient. They key factor here is time. Doctors, nurses and other healthcare staff are losing the time they need to be able to be there for their patients. As the good Samaritan study showed, when pressured by time we lose our tendency to be compassionate. Time is money, as the business world says.

Coming back to the arithmetic of compassion and how numbers can be deadly for our compassionate actions, removing barriers to help is an important consideration in dealing with mass suffering. We can make donating easier, offering the opportunity to donate regularly as opposed to as a once off, and we can use the identifiable victim effect strategically to encourage action. The media also has a role to play in the discourse around helping. News programs and newspapers can provide information on compassionate behaviours and suggest ways we can help. Framing narratives around how our sacrifices give others a chance to prosper can be important. Presently, our media is dominated by threat-based stories, often highlighting what we might lose rather than what we might gain in helping others.

Creating compassionate environments can help remove systemic and structural barries that inhibit compassion. Designing cities to be more conducive to compassion is one important consideration.[14] Another can be found in universities. Drs Theo Gilbert and Frances Maratos have examined how to create compassionate classrooms in the university environment, so students from culturally and linguistically diverse backgrounds feel included and accepted, instead of excluded.[15]

Slovic recommends a number of important decision aids to help avoid the collapse of compassion, and one suggestion is using performance measures that track changes.[16] How can you know you are helping if you aren't measuring it? Often we resign ourselves to vague goals, like 'promote humanitarian interventions', but we must be able to translate these goals to metrics that we can assess. Thankfully, though, there are incredible organisations that do this already, such as War Child, an organisation that supports children and young people affected by war. In groups like this, we see there is hope: people around the world are dedicating themselves to imagining and assessing new ways to invigorate and sustain our compassion to the immense suffering to which all life is vulnerable.

10

Compassionate contradictions

Humans are walking contradictions, and in our compassionate behaviour we're no different; we take actions to be compassionate, but still do other things that may cause suffering. For example, I love orangutans and donate money monthly to a charity in Borneo to help with orangutan conservation. I have been doing this for five years, yet until only recently I also used to cook with vegetable oil. Vegetable oil contains palm oil, which I didn't realise, and palm oil is the number one contributor to habitat destruction for orangutans in Borneo.

This is a classic example of a compassionate contradiction, when we do one thing aimed to help an entity, but then take other actions that undermine it or, at its worst, cause suffering instead. I was embarrassed when I found out vegetable oil contained palm oil. I even for a brief moment thought, 'What's the point of trying?' I suspect many can relate to this feeling, particularly when it comes to issues like climate change. We do things like switch our light bulbs over to more environmentally friendly ones, stop using plastic straws, get rid of single-use plastics and buy KeepCups for our coffee, and yet the Australian government continues to subsidise the fossil-fuel industry, and we are the second-largest exporter of coal in the world.

The fact of the matter is, humans are walking, talking contradictions. I think many Australians feel like we are good global citizens who care deeply for others, yet Australia's generosity measured by foreign aid as a share of national income has recently fallen significantly, from 0.36% to 0.23% (a cut of $1.6 billion), despite the United Nations' target being 0.7%.[1] Moreover, these cuts appear largely in line with the will of the people, with only 22% of Australians supporting a potential increase in foreign aid spending.[2] I am sure people in other countries view this as a contradiction. Many Australians would agree with this view, but others might also agree with the idea that we must care for ourselves before we care for others. Indeed, a recent president of the US campaigned on that exact premise; he even made hats.

Many believe you can't be compassionate to others before you are self-compassionate. But this is not true. It also misses the point that our first experience of compassion is not giving it or being self-compassionate, but receiving it from others. For many of us that would be from our parents. Research has found we can be good at giving compassion to others, but low in self-compassion and vice versa.[3] The Compassion Focused Therapy group workshops I ran for people with weight shame perfectly illustrated this compassionate contradiction. The group members were deeply compassionate to each other, but did not like receiving compassion. This in some ways is denying other people the opportunity of giving compassion, something we value.

We can examine our contradictions from many different perspectives, but one important point is to not police our actions or those of others. You might want to become a more compassionate person, but it is impossible to be compassionate at every minute of every hour of every day. There are other competing demands, like work, rest and play. If you are hyper-monitoring your compassionate actions, this can cause problems. If you have difficulty sleeping, one of the worst things you can do is to monitor whether you have fallen asleep yet. The continual checking keeps you aroused, which is the opposite physiological pattern to what is required for sleep. We can do this for our compassionate actions as well. 'Was that compassionate enough? Should I have done more? Have I done enough?' These questions can make us feel like we are in a competition, and the most compassionate wins.

There are many ways we can engage with compassion. For example, we can try to notice suffering in our homes, among our friends and in our communities, but we can also broaden our attention globally. Indeed, Australia is an affluent country with good health and education resources. Arguably the best way to maximise our compassionate footprint is to look beyond Australia and help people living in countries with heightened poverty, in danger zones or with poor access to health and education – those most vulnerable.

When we consider a relatively simple question such as, 'What is the most compassionate action I can take right now?' many of us can be left stumped. As a result, we can easily revert to what *feels* right. That is why communities like Effective Altruism exist, to take the guesswork out and minimise our emotional bias. But we don't have altruism algorithms at our fingertips when we encounter suffering in our everyday life. Rather we do the best we can in that moment. If our actions help the target, that is great. If not, at least we tried. Importantly, there is no final destination for compassion. After 10,000 acts of compassion or 10,000 hours of compassion meditation, we don't reach the end point of compassion and no longer need to do anything else. There is always more suffering. And critically, in the words of Fred Rogers, there are always people turning up to help.

I was reminded of our compassionate contradictions in the master's course I teach at the University of Queensland. In the course I train future psychologists to work effectively to improve the therapeutic relationship between psychologist and patient, as well as to identify and repair therapeutic ruptures. A rupture can be thought of as when the two parties, psychologist and patient, aren't on the same page. Sometimes you might not even know it. Ruptures can take the form of a disagreement over what the best goals in therapy are, or a patient being wary of speaking honestly to a psychologist. Psychologists might also cause ruptures in how we react and respond to a patient.

An example of one such rupture is minimising a client's emotional experience. For example, a patient might convey real distress and anxiety over an upcoming event, such as going to a party. A psychologist might reflect by saying, 'It sounds like you are a bit distressed.' The inclusion of 'a bit' minimises the emotional experience of the patient. But when I was teaching this to my students one said, 'I don't see it this way. The inclusion of "a bit", when I use it, is trying to be corrective for the patient, showing them that they can handle the emotional experience.' In other words, the student can see the patient is suffering, and tries to help by showing them they can handle the emotional experience by saying 'a bit', trying to give the patient a greater perspective. I understand the student's perspective, but my response to this is, yes, your intention might be to help your patient, but I don't think the other person experiences it that way. In other words, this is a compassionate contradiction: you're trying to help somebody but taking actions that undermine the intended help.

Imagine coming home from work after a stressful day, later than you'd planned, because the traffic was terrible. You walk in the door and say to your partner, 'It's been a shocking day, and to make matters worse I have another Zoom call to do tonight.' If your partner responds with 'It sounds like you are *a bit* stressed', you may react badly. You want to hear 'That sounds terrible'. You want your experience to be validated. Once we have been validated, we then soften and begin to consider other options. However, sometimes we can be so eager to help people we say or do things that can make the matter worse.

As discussed earlier, in my PhD research I ran groups with grandparents who provided regular childcare to their grandchildren. In the grandparent–parent literature there is a well-known double-bind effect.[4] This is when parents expect grandparents to be supportive without interfering. A tricky juggling act. Research shows that what parents dislike most about grandparent involvement is receiving unsolicited parenting advice from them, as it is seen as interfering and judgemental.[5] Grandparents know this, but can't help themselves and interfere anyway, believing that while the parents might not like hearing it now, they really need to know. But all the research shows that it's not worth it; it hurts the relationship. It increases the tension between the grandparent and parent, and it can result in the parents looking elsewhere for care.

We fall into this trap all the time. We argue with friends over politics, believing our facts will show them the folly of their beliefs and they will change their minds and agree with our worldview. What actually happens, however, is the other person becomes defensive and believes in their own position even more.[6] The strategy completely backfires. We are not very good at having discussions over ethical or moral issues where there can be disagreements. We can easily and quickly move into attack and defend positions, taking things personally or trying to win the argument instead of trying to understand the many different layers to an issue. It seems in some ways we have lost the art of good conversation: being able to talk about real issues, having disagreements, trying to open our minds to differences, all while still liking and respecting each other. One view doesn't make a person. Yet, when we watch political debates, more often than not we hear yelling and personal attacks, rather than purposeful, considered, thoughtful discussion. It's almost like conversation has turned into something to be won, instead of a medium through which to exchange ideas.

The other aspect to compassionate contradictions is they can make compassion feel like a 'holier than thou' position, or the moral high ground. People can feel like their compassionate actions or inaction are being policed. Take vegetarianism or veganism. Anecdotally I hear of many people who have completed a formal compassion-based program deciding to shift to a plant-based diet. There can be several reasons for this, but there is good research showing becoming vegetarian or vegan has a positive environmental impact,[7] and given other sentient beings, like animals, can suffer, if we take a compassionate approach to all life that might mean stopping eating meat.

This philosophy was catapulted into popular culture by Peter Singer in his seminal book, *Animal Liberation*. The basis of his push to stop factory farming and the consumption of meat is utilitarianism. The philosophical idea is that we should maximise utility, or in other words happiness or pleasure, and avoid actions that cause harm. As a result, utilitarianism is very concerned with the effects of our actions. The central point of Singer's argument is that humans might have greater complexity when it comes to cognition, but all animals can suffer and experience pain. You might experience transient happiness eating your eye fillet, but the suffering of the cow is deemed to be greater. As such the most utilitarian act is to stop eating eye fillets. There are many other dimensions – the land cleared for cattle grazing, the water used to grow grain and so on – which all contribute to the cost of beef, and the idea is that these resources could be used more effectively.

One of my colleagues, Emily, had a similar experience. She had completed several compassion meditation retreats and was now researching morality, and she said she just started to become uncomfortable with the idea of saying one thing ('Compassion and reducing suffering is important') and doing another (eating meat). This is sometimes referred to as 'cognitive dissonance': a mental conflict when our behaviours and beliefs don't align. There are many ways of managing this conflict, but the action Emily took was to stop eating meat. What's annoying about this? Well, after being vegetarian for a few years, she then read some research that suggests if you want to help reduce the suffering of cows it could be better to go off dairy than red meat.[8] It was another one of those 'What's the point of even trying?' moments. She now drinks oat milk.

All of these changes were fundamentally about how my friend Emily saw her beliefs and actions, not how others saw them. Yet she couldn't help but feel that her friends were annoyed with her when she went to social gatherings and parties. She said she would often get asked why she went off meat. At first, she would say because she thought it was better for the environment or that she struggled with the idea of killing animals. The response she would get was 'Yes, but you still drive a car that runs on petrol. That's bad for the environment.' Or 'Are you saying I'm a bad person for eating meat? Humans were designed to eat meat.' Of course she was saying neither, but her friends felt threatened and were defensive, attempting to reject her ideas.

Thankfully there has been some research unpacking these kind of dilemmas. In one study, Drs Julia Minson and Benoît Monin asked participants to write down any three words they associated with veganism.[9] All up, 47% of the respondents wrote something negative, and 45% included a word that described a person's characteristics, such as 'weird', 'arrogant' or 'militant'. It is no wonder then that vegans often feel negatively judged.

Another study, by Drs Cara MacInnis and Gordon Hodson, found that omnivores evaluated vegetarians and vegans more negatively than those in other nutritional groups, such as people with gluten intolerances.[10] Moreover, those who were motivated to be vegan or vegetarian because of animal rights or environmental concerns were the most negatively evaluated.

But why do omnivores judge vegetarians and vegans so negatively? Drs Matthew Ruby and Steven Heine might have an answer to this question.[11] They found that those who self-reported being vegetarian felt they were morally superior to those who described themselves as omnivores. Omnivores also said vegetarians were significantly more virtuous. This sense of moral superiority is off-putting. What this research also suggests is what we choose to eat is linked to our sense of identity.

One study has found that men who are vegetarian are perceived as less masculine compared to men who eat meat, because masculinity is associated with meat.[12] What this points to is how quick we are to discriminate against people. We'll discriminate based on anything and everything, including people's diet. Researchers have found that those considering turning to a more plant-based diet fear the stigma that comes with it. They specifically fear people such as family and friends hating them, to the point that it can stop them from making the change.[13] We tend to love farm animals, and we even glorify them in children's books, yet it seems we only love them and farm them to eat them. If we didn't eat them, would we love them?

Human ingenuity is leading to inventions that enable those who enjoy the taste of meat to continue to do so guilt-free. Scientists have invented cultivated meat, grown in a lab. The process involves extracting a cell from the fat or muscle from a cow, for example, and putting that cell into a cultured medium that feeds it, allowing it to multiply. It is extraordinary. No harm is done to life, and you can still eat your BBQ meat guilt-free. The cultivated meat process was very expensive initially, with one article reporting that the cost of a cultivated beef burger was approximately $250,000 less than ten years ago. But the costs have dropped dramatically to a very affordable $10.[14] Richard Dawkins even tweeted that this technology might lead to an end to the taboo of cannibalism, as you could eat human meat without cost of life. (Taking this idea a step further, as a thought experiment, it could lead to a whole celebrity meat market where you could buy a Brad Pitt burger using the same processes. Extract his cell, grow it, and then eat it in a burger. Brad makes a bit of money, and we enjoy a bit of Brad.)

What is interesting in this argument about eating animals is that as humans we have the cognitive capacity to dream of possible alternatives. We used to hunt animals, then we farmed them, and now we are even growing meat in labs. Other animals do not have these options. A lion cannot wake up one day and think to itself how sad it is that it eats baby zebras and so decide to go vegetarian. Even if a lion could do this, its digestive tract wouldn't be able to break down a vegetarian diet; it needs meat. But humans have robust digestive systems that can break down many foods. We have also evolved an advanced style of cooking, which has allowed us to create a totally different way of thinking about and consuming food. Abilities like these are what make us such a powerful compassionate species. We can use our creativity and cognitive capacities to reduce suffering not just for humans but for all life.

There has been a lot of research into our attitudes towards different diets, like veganism and vegetarianism, hence why I have discussed it here. It isn't to convince you to become a vegan or vegetarian. There are many pathways to living a more sustainable lifestyle that is good for sentient beings and the environment. But with the busyness of everyday life it is easy to avoid asking ourselves if we can make any small changes to benefit others. So often we are consumed with how our decisions affect ourselves, we don't think outwards about how these decisions affect others.

I was once at a compassion workshop at the University of Edinburgh where we were discussing power and leadership. One question posed was, 'What would you be willing to sacrifice to allow someone less privileged than you a chance for something more?' Research by Professor Dacher Keltner and others has unfortunately consistently found that the more power we get the harder we find it is to make these sacrifices, often rewarding ourselves for our efforts.[15]

If we leave responsibility solely to the individual it makes it difficult for more compassionate societies to be realised. Despite what I may ideally want, I know I am going to be biased towards my own family and friends in times of need. This is part of being human. I'm a walking, talking contradiction. That is why many global issues like poverty and climate change need organisations and regulations in place to provide the structure for a compassionate way of living. That is why organisations such as the United Nations came into existence, to promote peace and security between nations.

Another organisation that aims to create more compassionate societies is Compassion in Politics in the UK. Co-Founder Jennifer Nadel has spoken about how they are trying to get politicians to agree not to pass any legislation that would knowingly hurt or harm the most vulnerable groups. Unfortunately, governments around the world have knowingly hurt the most vulnerable groups time and again. In Australia, for example, the 'robodebt' scheme, which ran from 2015 to 2019, saw the government unlawfully raise $1.76 billion in debts against 443,000 people as part of a welfare debt recovery program. The judge ruling on the case pointed out that this welfare debt recovery was targeted at the most marginalised and vulnerable. Moreover, the judge also said that it should have been obvious to ministers and public servants involved that this was a flawed scheme. That is why we have groups like Compassion in Politics trying to improve our systems.

Finally, one other difficulty we have to contend with when it comes to our compassionate contradictions is the phenomenon of moral licensing. This is a phenomenon in which we believe our past good deeds 'allow' us the chance to engage in actions that are immoral, unethical or otherwise problematic.[16] This is subconscious for the most part. For example, someone might work large amounts of overtime for their employer, so feel comfortable taking home office supplies for their personal use, despite it being stealing. Adopting a more compassionate focus, another person might feel that given they donate a lot of time volunteering for charities, it's okay for them to claim some extra hours at work, despite not doing them. It's an internal bargaining system we have, and we'd be ashamed if others knew about it. One classic study found that those who voted for President Obama were likely to be racist or prejudiced afterwards.[17] We can fall into this trap with our compassionate contradictions.

Trying to be more compassionate to others and ourselves is a goal many of us share. It is tricky though; sometimes we can feel we are doing more harm than good. We might purchase ethically, register as an organ donor, donate blood, do a compassion meditation – we might even spend time volunteering to help others who are suffering. We can do all these amazing acts, but in other areas, even unbeknown to us, we are causing harm. Reflecting on what factors lead us to decide to be compassionate or not can help open up new thoughts and ideas about our behaviours and what we choose to do.

The Dalai Lama has said that because he is a Buddhist monk and meditates every day, focusing on compassion constantly, people often think that he must be a calm and content person. But he says, just like everyone else, he is also human and can feel angry or get upset. We will never be perfect. There is no perfect compassion, just our genuine attempts to be helpful. And taking small steps towards this intention is what is most important. A great example: in 1970 around 20 million children were dying each year around the world because of poverty. That number has dropped to 5 million today.[18] What extraordinary progress. There is still so much to do, but if we put our collective minds to it, anything is possible.

11

Compassion around the world

You are blind and need to cross the street. Out of all the cities in all the world, in which would you be most likely to get help? Would it be amid the hustle and bustle of New York City? Or on the streets of Kolkata? Perhaps Kuala Lumpur would be better?

It turns out, the city where you would be most likely to receive help is Rio de Janeiro, Brazil.

Say it was something more ordinary; say you dropped your pen when crossing the street. Where would you be most likely to get help from a stranger? The answer is the same, Rio. Ramping up the suffering, imagine you are wearing a leg brace and you accidentally drop the pile of magazines you're carrying. In which city is it most likely you'll get help?

The answer for a third time is Rio. When you are in the need of help from strangers, Peter Allen was right: go to Rio.

These are the clever helping-behaviour field experiments Drs Robert Levine, Ara Norenzayan and Karen Philbrick conducted across 23 large cities around the world in 2001.[1] The aim of their experiments was to get some insight into whether cross-cultural differences exist in the types of spontaneous, non-emergency helping you see in everyday life. Rio came first, with San José in Costa Rica and Lilongwe in Malawi rounding out the top three. The bottom three were Singapore, New York and Kuala Lampur. At the top of the table, helping behaviour occurred at a frequency of about 80% and higher. For the bottom three cities, helping dropped to around 40%.

The good news from these experiments is that even in big cities for the most part we are pretty helpful, with the top 20 cities always helping at a rate of 50% or higher across the three behavioural measures. But why do we see such a magnitude of difference between some of these countries? The authors examined some key factors, such as actual population size, walking speed (a measure of the pace of life) and, as an economic indicator, purchasing power parity (in other words, average citizen wealth calculated from GDP). Out of all these factors the only one that correlated with helping behaviour was wealth, with a negative correlation; that is, the wealthier the city the less likely it was to be helpful. Interestingly, one cultural factor was key: *simpatia* cultures were far more likely to help than those countries without that tradition.

Simpatia cultures are defined by their proactive socio-emotional orientation and concern for the social wellbeing of others. Countries with a *simpatia* culture in this study included Brazil, Costa Rica, El Salvador and Mexico. In these cultures there is an implicit prerogative to be actively friendly, polite and helpful towards strangers. No surprises then that it was in countries with this cultural orientation that helping was the highest. But this raises the critical question: what do we mean by culture?

Culture has many definitions. A useful way to think about it is as the shared meanings and activities that meet the ecological demands and social structure of the environment.[2] You can think of micro levels of cultures (families), meso levels of culture (neighbourhoods, workplaces, schools), and macro levels (government, laws, economy, politics – factors that shape a country). A culture can remain quite stable over time, such as *simpatia* cultures, or we can try to create a specific type of culture in newly formed groups, families, schools or companies. This can be done through top-down processes (enforced from the hierarchy – rules or policies) or bottom-up processes (coming from the community). Through either of these processes, cultures can change quickly and dynamically.

When it comes to the science of compassion, we have mostly studied people who come from Western cultures. This is a problem. In fact, there is an acronym in psychology, coined by Dr Joseph Henrich, WEIRD, which refers to Western Educated Industrialised Rich Democratic populations.[3] Most of the psychology studies I have described across these chapters come from populations that could be described as WEIRD. Although there are many strengths to research in psychology, our understanding of complex constructs is generally limited to WEIRD cultural backgrounds. The simple truth is we just haven't done enough research with diverse backgrounds to truly understand how compassion is experienced and expressed in different cultures.

I was confronted with this reality when I travelled to Japan to run a series of compassion workshops. We were presenting to about 350 Japanese clinical psychologists, and we were presenting in English. It was all translated by a team of three translators who were also psychologists. It was made clear to us very early on the first day that there is no direct translation for compassion in Japanese. The closest translation we had was *omoiyari*. *Omoi* means being considerate and caring for others, while *yari* means sending something to others. Therefore, *omoiyari* literally means sending one's altruistic feelings to others. This is very similar to the Western definition of compassion, which is 'having a sensitivity to suffering in self and others, with a commitment to try to alleviate it'. But it is also different in some fundamental ways. *Omoiyari* lacks the behavioural action component of compassion, and the explicit focus on suffering is absent. Thus, how we understand compassion and compassionate behaviour in Japanese cultures will be slightly different to how we understand it in English-speaking cultures. In Japan, we unexpectedly had to spend quite a bit of time in the workshop discussing these differences in what we mean by compassion, as there were moments of understandable confusion.

The most common dimension of culture many of us know is the continuum from collectivism to individualism. Collectivistic cultures tend to emphasise the needs and goals of the group as a whole over the needs and desires of each individual. Examples are countries such as Japan, China, Indonesia and India. On the other hand, individualistic cultures tend to stress the needs of the individual over the needs of the group, suggesting that we tend to be more independent and autonomous, having our own attitudes and preferences. Countries that have a more individualistic framework include the US, Germany and Australia. Interestingly, this dimension of culture did not significantly influence whether strangers helped in the studies by Levine, Norenzayan and Philbrick.

In contrast to what you might expect, the US was found to be the most compassionate country in 2019 using another metric of compassion. But how? This metric is called the World Giving Index and is calculated by an organisation called Charities Aid Foundation (CAF).[4] In this index, individuals are asked three questions about helpful behaviours: over the past month, have they helped a stranger or someone they didn't know who needed help, donated money to a charity, or volunteered their time to an organisation.

In countries that are more individualistic, people believe it is important to have the agency to decide who to help. Research has shown that we tend to donate to charities and help causes that are emotionally close to us and relevant to us. For example, my grandmother lost her life to breast cancer, and as a result I donate to breast cancer charities. But why breast cancer and not prostate cancer or infectious disease or something else entirely? My number one reason to donate to this cause is because I have been personally impacted by it.

The metrics used to calculate the World Giving Index are geared more towards individualistic cultural views (hardly surprising given the organisation is based in the UK), hence why countries such as the US have long topped the rankings. However, this index does not consider how much money people would be willing to be taxed to be redistributed by government for causes such as welfare, education, health and housing. On those indices the US would not rank as highly.

Interestingly, in the 2021 report, which collected data in 2020 from over 114,000 people from 114 countries, there was a massive change in the rankings, with Indonesia being ranked most generous (69%), followed by Kenya (58%) and Nigeria (52%). Australia ranked fifth (49%) and US dropped to 19th (43%). The percentages reflect how many of those surveyed reported saying yes to donating, helping and volunteering. Why did the US drop so significantly? According to CAF, it was because of COVID-19. The data was collected during the first year of the pandemic, when many Western countries were experiencing restrictions such as lockdowns, which led to reductions in individual helping. But how did Australia remain robust to this effect, given the city of Melbourne holds the record for longest COVID-19 lockdown? The report indicates that it is likely Australia remained robust because of the incredible generous financial response to the bushfires we had in early 2020.

The report concludes that although there was a significant drop in generosity in a number of countries, it wasn't because people didn't want to help, but rather that people lost the opportunity. This is interesting, because although lockdowns and restrictions reduced the opportunities for individual generosity as calculated by these three measures, many lives were saved due to the same restrictions. Staying home is a significant cost, yet we did it on scale to protect others. That is compassion, but metrics such as the World Giving Index miss these nuances.

Another way to conceptualise culture is as tight or loose.[5] Tight cultures tend to have strong norms and low tolerance for deviant behaviour (e.g., Japan), whereas loose cultures have weak norms and high tolerance for deviant behaviour (e.g., Netherlands). Dr Michele Gelfand and colleagues suggest that how we respond to strong or weak everyday situations is influenced by whether we live in a tight or loose culture. For example, in weak everyday situations there is a lack of external pressures, like regulations, which allows for a range of behaviours as responses. In strong everyday situations there are high levels of regulation and a restricted range of appropriate behaviour. It is suggested that there is an expectation in tight cultures that you act with higher constraints in everyday situations than in loose cultures.

Imagine you are watching an elderly person crossing the street very slowly with some obvious difficulty. In a tight culture you might not interfere, as it might be more appropriate to allow the individual the dignity, autonomy and agency to do it themselves.

In loose cultures you might be more likely to go and help the elderly person cross the street, even ignoring their protests, as you recognise they are just being nice and they really could do with the help. This model aligns with findings we discussed at the beginning of this chapter on helping strangers cross the street, as Gelfand and colleagues calculated that Brazil has a low score of 3.5, making it a loose culture, whereas Malaysia has a high score of 11.8, which makes them a very tight culture. And Malaysia ranked lowest in helping strangers cross the street, whereas Brazil was ranked the highest.

It is not the case that any culture is 'better' for compassion. The context of the perceived suffering is critically important. There is an ethical question here, though: should we in Western cultures be going into tight and collectivistic cultures trying to increase compassionate behaviour? There are many instances of Westerners bringing something they believe is good to a different culture with very bad outcomes. This has happened time and time again in Australian Indigenous communities, where Western-developed interventions have been imposed without cultural sensitivity. We have to be better and more attuned to the important role of culture when understanding the experience and expression of compassion.

My colleague Professor James Bennett-Levy from the University of Sydney experienced this when evaluating Compassion Focused Therapy with Indigenous Australians.[6] In the first instance he and his team ran the intervention as it was originally developed, and it came to nothing. There was no engagement in it whatsoever. The program was just not culturally suitable for Indigenous Australians in its current form. To fix this, James and his team ran a series of focus groups with the participants and a number of Indigenous researchers. They asked the participants what a better and more appropriate way to do this kind of program would look like, and whether it could even be useful at all. The responses were overwhelmingly constructive. This led to the program being delivered in a completely different way, with the facilitator being paired with a professional artist, and the participants given the opportunity to paint and draw their experiences of compassion and related concepts. This form of delivery led to the group members talking openly about their experiences, which was the exact opposite to the original format where nobody wanted to talk at all.

The research team renamed the program Arts-Based Compassion Skills Training, and the program evaluation concluded that creating a positive group atmosphere and channelling compassion skills training through the medium of visual arts led to four positive outcomes: planting the seeds of new understandings, embodying the skills of compassion, strengthening relationships, and developing a more self-compassionate relationship. Even though we are becoming an increasingly globalised world, we must remember there are fundamental differences in our cultural values that we must respect to better understand each other and consequently be helpful.

About three years ago I was at lunch with Dr Tony Fernando from the University of Auckland. He is a psychiatrist, as well as a Buddhist monk, a cellist and an open ocean swimmer. At this lunch he was telling me that he was thinking of returning to Bhutan. Tony had done many retreats and spent many years in Bhutan, and he told me that it's such a peaceful place that it was recently ranked the world's happiest country. Bhutan is a Buddhist kingdom, and is similar to New Zealand in terms of being a visually stunning country, with dramatic landscapes and mountains and valleys. He explained that in Bhutan children value all walks of life and will go out of their way to protect even the smallest creatures, such as ants, from the rain. These children are taught ethics first and then later shown how mindfulness can support their ethical teachings. In the West we do things slightly differently; in fact, the opposite. For the most part our mindfulness is taught with ethics stripped out.

In Bhutan the children don't protect the ants because they are being mindful, but rather their ethical principles lead them to act, and we do see similar acts in the West. Research by my colleague Dr Matti Wilks is showing that young children really value the life of other animals and plants, sometimes more so than other humans.[7] Ultimately they don't want anyone to get hurt or suffer. Indeed, children can become upset when they understand we kill and eat the animals they love.

This brings up an important point: do children in Bhutan experience and express compassion differently to children in Australia? One of my collaborators, Mark Nielsen, examines cross-cultural prosociality in children. He and others have done critical work in examining prosocial behaviour with children from various cultural backgrounds such as Western, Indigenous Australian, African hunter-gatherer and Tibetan.

One of the difficult things about doing this type of work is making the experimental tasks easy to demonstrate without needing language. Mark and I were working on adapting our existing experimental paradigm, which examines compassionate responding in childhood, so that it would be more cross-culturally friendly. Our task as it was involved a lot of verbal instructions. When we were deliberating how to modify the task Mark and I discussed a lot of research that had tried to do something similar. What we were struck by is that even what we think to be prosocial behaviour differs quite a lot between cultures.

Children's prosocial behaviour is shaped greatly by their opportunities to observe, participate in and learn from the chores and responsibilities that affect the adults around them. In some rural non-Western cultures, children are expected to help (e.g., carry firewood) as soon as they are able to walk, and by ages four to five are doing household duties like gardening and herding livestock. These behaviours make it seem as if children from these cultural backgrounds are extremely helpful.

In Western cultures we are far more focused on children learning skills for educational purposes, such as reading and writing, as opposed to taking on chores and responsibilities to contribute significantly to the running of the house. These parents would also likely describe these behaviours as prosocial;[8] however, the Western definition of prosocial behaviour is that it is voluntary and designed to help another.[9] Following parents' instructions or complying with their wants does not fit this definition, despite the helpfulness of the behaviours.

Thus, there are some cultural differences in how we come to understand prosocial behaviour – although I am sure many parents in Western cultures would be very happy if their children followed instructions more often.

Researchers have also looked at the concept of fairness across cultures, finding that Western children tend to redistribute spoils from a joint enterprise based on contribution, with those who did more work receiving more of the rewards.[10] This pattern does not emerge in other cultures. Children from a Kenyan pastoralist society didn't take merit into account at all, and a Namibian egalitarian hunter-gatherer group distributed the spoils more equally than the other two cultures. One reason proposed by the authors for these differences could be that in smaller-scale societies the personal relationships between members will be more long-term in nature, and are therefore more important than merit and equity within a single interaction.

This leads us to the work of Dr Nadia Chernyak and her team who have done groundbreaking research examining children's prosocial behaviour in Zambia.[11] Work done with WEIRD populations has found that children by age three show a variety of prosocial behaviour, such as helping, comforting and sharing. Chernyak and her team examined whether this type of prosocial behaviour also occurred with children raised in Zambia, a lower-middle-income country with high wealth inequality. They tested 370 children and found almost identical patterns of helping behaviour to what we would expect from a WEIRD sample. That is, children tended to be helpful and comforting, but when it came to sharing resources with a high cost, children helped significantly less. This is only one experimental study, but it shows some of the universality of compassion and prosocial helping across cultures. We are very helpful as a species, regardless of where we are raised.

One interesting aspect to Chernyak and her team's work is they also found that costly helping was positively correlated with parents who reported reading storybooks to their children. They concluded that children may draw upon their experience with stories as representations of real-life events. This finding is similar to other correlational cross-cultural research that finds reading fictional stories to children is associated with their development of empathy.[12]

Adults can also benefit from reading and improving their levels of empathy. A study published in the prestigious journal *Science* by Drs David Kidd and Emanuele Castano assigned participants to a condition of reading either literary fiction, genre fiction, non-fiction or nothing.[13] The researchers found those who read literary fiction experienced a significant increase in empathy, and those assigned to read non-fiction, genre fiction, or nothing had no boost at all to their empathy. So if you want to improve your empathy put this book down and pick up Jane Austen's *Emma*.

Immediately on reading this research you are struck by the thought of, what books am I reading? And equally, what books am I reading to my children? Some psychologists suggest it is better for us to read stories such as those by Danish author Hans Christian Andersen, as opposed to stories that always end happily ever after. In Andersen's stories there can be happy but also very unhappy endings, and this provides the child with multiple perspectives and emotional experiences. If we read stories that always end with the fairytale happily ever after, this narrows the emotional experience and children miss hearing about the different life experiences people have.

Stories are a very powerful medium for learning and education, and it might be possible that for children compassion can be best taught through stories. I am currently doing work with Dr Frankie Fong where we are examining whether books that convey compassionate actions lead to increased compassionate behaviour in four-year-olds.

Mark and I still haven't managed to successfully vary our experiment examining compassionate responding in young children to conduct experiments cross-culturally. It is something we hope to do in the future. But these cultural differences in prosocial behaviour reiterate the importance of understanding that there are many ways of being compassionate. It seems for the most part that compassionate and prosocial motivations are universal, but how this manifests into behaviour depends on culture. Hardly a surprise, but something we can forget easily in this globalised world.

12

The future of compassion

There is an animated film called *Big Hero 6* that tells the story of a computer engineer who creates a robot healthcare worker. The robot is deliberately programmed to show compassion when their patient is sad.

Would you like to be cared for by a robot programmed to show compassion? I am ambivalent about this, but people I have spoken to have firm views. One group see it is as a serious problem, with responses like, 'We have lost our humanity.' The other group think it's a blessing, as so many people are lonely and in need of some form of care. Personally, as a psychologist, I like to think talking with a person, another human mind, makes a difference, but does it? Are robot therapists the way of the future?

One study examined this very question. They asked whether 'virtual humans', when designed to be supportive and safe, are more effective at eliciting self-disclosure and true emotional experience from patients than humans.[1] Being truthful and honest about one's experiences and symptoms are critical factors in health care; as such there might be advantages in virtual humans if they elicit true experience better than, dare I say it, 'normal' humans. In this study, participants interacted with a virtual human on a monitor screen, which they believed was being operated by either a human or by automation. The virtual human asked participants eight questions about personal factors, such as 'Tell me about the hardest decision you've ever had to make', 'Tell me about an event, or something that you wish you could erase from your memory' and 'What's something you feel guilty about?' During the interview, the virtual human followed up comments with 'Can you tell me about that?' Critically, the virtual human also provided verbal empathic feedback such as 'I'm sorry to hear that', as well as nodding and showing a range of different expressions to convey active and empathic listening.

The authors of this study were clever. They informed the participants that the virtual human was controlled by a real human or by automation, but some participants were misled. For example, they were told they were with a virtual human controlled by a human when it was actually controlled by automation, and vice versa.

After the interview the participants were asked a number of things, including whether they believed the virtual human was controlled by a person or by automation. The study design helped remove social desirability bias that could unintentionally impact the answer to this question. The researchers were also interested in the level of fear participants had in disclosing information, their level of impression management (disclosing information that might lead others to view them positively), and the intensity of their sadness displayed during the interview.

What did they find? Believe it or not, participants who believed they were interacting with a virtual human controlled by automation reported lower fears of self-disclosure, lower impression management, and they displayed their sadness more intensely. The authors interpreted these findings as showing that if people believe no other human is observing them they feel safer to express themselves honestly. And some of the quotes from the study clearly support this view: 'This is way better than talking to a person. I don't really feel comfortable talking about personal stuff to other people.' And 'A human being would be judgemental. I shared a lot of personal things, and it was because of that.'

To those who see the positives of robots and artificial intelligence (AI), the results from this study are probably unsurprising. But to those who are more sceptical, these results might get you to rethink your position. There are some contexts where robots and AI are very helpful, but in other situations, although they might be helpful, we get a gut feeling that it isn't right or appropriate. I guess the question is: do we want to live in the kind of world where we are cared for by non-living things?

This is an emotionally intense issue in Australia, as a recent royal commission uncovered details of how individuals in aged care have been horribly treated. Older adults in aged care are vulnerable people and vulnerability usually triggers a compassionate response. Yet the aged-care system has been failing them. The royal commission found that there have been high levels of neglect and that the system has not delivered safe and quality care. How do we fix this? The movie *Big Hero 6* provides one possible solution: with technology. It is almost impossible to argue against the idea that robots programmed to be compassionate might be better for older adults than the care they are receiving currently by humans.

But, while integrating robots and AI into health care might be part of the answer, I don't think it is the solution to all our problems. Many of us might object to the idea of being cared for by robots and AI, perhaps even harbouring the fear that they could turn against us. A fair point. Humans have been hurting each other for millennia, though. My objection to robots and AI is not on these grounds; rather, I don't think we can receive the kind of compassion from a robot that we receive from humans. And that matters.

When we are compassionate to another person, we typically try to empathise with their situation. We try to understand their perspective and get a sense of their emotional experience, their life story. This is both effortful and unpleasant at times, as the emotions experienced can be difficult. It takes courage to be compassionate towards others; we take on costs such as effort and distressing emotions, and it also requires making sacrifices, such as giving up time. During COVID-19, many healthcare workers have taken huge risks, even giving their lives, to help people who desperately need care. Receiving that kind of care from another human can be transformative. The intention itself can be transformative. It provides a sense of togetherness, solidarity, belonging, a feeling that we are living in a community that cares for each other. These feelings are not trivial. Research has found time and again that a sense of belonging is crucial for our health.[2] We will never get that from a robot, as they don't feel those things or make those sacrifices. Rather, they are programmed to act out the algorithms that make them function.

We can empathise with other human minds because we ourselves have human minds, and we can understand how our minds get caught up in all sorts of trouble, thinking worst possible outcomes, fantasising, monitoring what other people think of us and feeling inferior. A mind has fears and hopes and dreams. Robots can't empathise with that human experience.

By way of example, I often teach a therapeutic technique to my students called 'empathic bodily reflection'. When expressing my empathy towards a patient for their situation I can do that with words, but I can also express that with my body.

A client, Hina, was telling me of her difficulties as a working single mother with three children, and how it was weighing on her. She felt trapped. Hina was a stoic woman and rarely showed emotion in our sessions. She would often say how she needed to keep things together for everyone: be the composed one, the responsible one. But she felt terrible for feeling trapped by her children, because having children is what she had desperately wanted in life and she thought she should feel lucky to have them. Compounding matters, she would say how terrible it would be if her kids knew she felt trapped by them. She said, 'What kind of mother would they think I am if I told them I feel trapped by them and get annoyed by having to look after them all the time?'

At this point, I could have given an empathic verbal reflection, conveying the deep sadness she was experiencing, as well as shame. But instead, I gave an empathic bodily reflection, which was, 'As you said that, Hina, I felt my whole body just sink into the chair, as if there is a great weight on me that I can barely hold and carry, a weight that I want to just throw away.' As I said this I was moving my body, sinking into the chair and then throwing my arms up to convey the throwing away of weight.

At this, Hina broke down into tears, something she had not done in our previous three sessions. I had connected with her, not by relying on my words, but by showing her how these emotions impacted my body. After the crying stopped there was a period of silence. Hina relaxed into her chair by leaning back into it, whereas she usually sat upright, and she commented, 'It's strange, but I feel like the weight is a little lighter now.'

A robot might be able to verbalise empathic responses, as happened in the study with virtual humans, but a robot can't feel how these emotions and thoughts ripple through our bodies in quite the same way a human can. Humans are designed to respond to the sounds, touch, sights, tastes and smells of other humans, something robots can't fathom, because they aren't moved by these senses in the same ways we are. The inverse of this might be seeing a distressed sea turtle caught in a net in the ocean. We want to calm it, so we stroke it and reassure it with our tone of voice, saying, 'It's okay. We're going to help you.' The sea turtle doesn't find these efforts of ours calming; turtles do not have the physiological infrastructure of humans, so they don't respond to touch and reassuring tones like we would. The only thing that will calm the sea turtle is to escape and be alone again, away from the net and from humans.

Like touch, sounds also have a significant impact on our feelings. Dr James Doty from Stanford University wrote that 'the first sounds we hear in this world are the heartbeats of our mother'. When we have children, we try to reassure them and play with them using friendly tones of voice. Despite many of us not being excellent singers, parents all around the world sing to their children when they are distressed to calm them. It doesn't always work, but it often does. In times of stress it's common to turn to music. Associate Professor Genevieve Dingle has found in her research that listening to music has a valuable role in regulating our emotional experiences throughout life.[3]

Robots and AI do not have these human senses or understand what it feels like to experience these senses. We can program certain features in. We can even turn a decision-making model of compassion into an algorithm such that AI makes the optimal decision each time it is confronted with suffering. But this isn't the same as hearing the voice of your mother or your son. Perhaps most importantly, robots and AI do not have the capacity to have a meta-awareness of who and what they are. For example, I have thoughts, but I am also aware that it is me who is having the thoughts. As Descartes famously said, 'I think, therefore I am.' We don't see that kind of meta-awareness in other technologies nor, to the best of our knowledge, in other living creatures.

I think we can only consider compassion as being in the realm of sentient creatures. As sentient beings, we know we have finite lives; we will grow, hopefully flourish, but also eventually age, decay and die. Our time on this Earth is limited and we know it. Thus, our lives have suffering built in, and we are aware that we suffer. Compassion is focused on trying as best we can to alleviate the suffering of other sentient beings. Robots and AI do not operate in this realm. They are not sentient, so cannot suffer, and without consciousness they cannot have an awareness of suffering. Rather, they are trained to respond in a certain way to signals in their environment. They aren't aware they are doing these things; it is simply programmed in. They are like central heating, monitoring the temperature of the room and turning on if it drops to a certain level. It is the same as a robot saying 'I'm sorry to hear that' when it detects you are sad. There might be a compassionate intention from the engineer who designed the algorithm, but the AI is working on programming, not compassion.

Looking at it another way: I might really love my car and care for it a great deal, spending lots of time and money cleaning it and making sure it works smoothly. But if my car were to be damaged, I wouldn't feel sympathy for it, because my car does not have feelings. Nor would I feel like I should be compassionate towards my car and alleviate its suffering, as it doesn't suffer. I would get the car repaired, as I like it and I need it, but that's it.

I think the same holds for robots and AI. When we program robots and AI to be caring, they are sometimes referred to as 'carebots', and there are many hundreds of carebot apps available. Research shows that apps like these can be helpful for mental health,[4] but I don't think they are a replacement for human-to-human interaction and compassion.

Compassion does not simply go one way, either. It is interactional. Giving and receiving compassion from each other can be a rewarding, meaningful and even pleasurable experience. There can be a warm glow after we are compassionate towards someone. This is a lovely design feature in humans, that we feel good when we help someone. If robots and AI were to do all our compassion work for us, we might lose this warm glow.

And can robots and AI really be programmed to be compassionate? Who are the people creating these algorithms? Do they fully understand what compassion is? These are questions that Dr Shannon Vallor from the University of Edinburgh has posed in her research examining technology and virtues.[5] Research shows that AI is biased, as humans create it and we are biased. It is impossible to disentangle the two. Moreover, a lot of machine-learning code is written by white men,[6] which brings in another level of bias, and also shows the lack of cultural diversity currently in the system. In many senses, the way we talk about AI and the future of a robot world is not at all matched by the reality in which we live. There is still a long way to go. However, we must have these conversations as technology continues to creep more and more into our daily lives.

The big question for us to tackle is: what kind of future world do we want to live in? How should we create it? Do we want to live in a world where every time we are upset, sad or disenchanted we have a carebot saying to us, 'I'm sorry to hear that'?

Casting our minds back to *Good Will Hunting*, there is a scene in which Chuckie (played by Ben Affleck) gets angry with Will for not taking a chance on a new life with a new job using his gifts. Chuckie even goes so far as to say that he'd kill Will if he didn't take this opportunity. This scene is powerfully compassionate, because Chuckie knows he will never have the opportunity that Will has to get out of this life and live something better. How frustrating to see his best friend too scared to take that chance.

This reaction from Chuckie is a powerful demonstration of compassion. It isn't soothing; it is assertive and energising. How do you program that into AI? In this interaction, Chuckie is showing an incredibly deep level of empathy and compassion towards Will, and Will gets it – you can see it in his face. Hearing this message from Chuckie is infinitely more powerful than anything delivered from AI, because Chuckie has a human mind and he shows his vulnerability, something AI cannot do. But who knows, maybe one day this kind of interacting and connecting will be programmed into AI.

Our futures are going to include greater integration of technologies and AI. There is no disputing that. Besides, there are many ways we can use these technologies to reduce suffering. But they aren't compassionate themselves. They also must be regulated, as there is the potential for a myriad of problems with privacy and misinformation, which are already widespread and deeply problematic on social media platforms.

Still, there are some extraordinary ways technologies are being used. A colleague of mine in the UK, Dr Tim Anstiss, is using virtual technologies on palliative care wards so patients in hospitals who cannot leave can see and experience what it is like to be at the beach again, hearing the sounds of the waves and seeing the blueness of the ocean. This provides great respite and calm for patients, as hospital settings tend to be bland and sterile.

One of my patients, who was coming to therapy for depression, had a grandmother she was extremely close to in palliative care. My patient, Jill, was with her grandmother constantly and described the room she was in as bleak. The room was big, but it didn't have a TV and it was dark. The windows looked out onto another bland orange-brick building, and you couldn't see the sky. Jill said, 'I was depressed already, but then going into that sterile, dark, boring room where my grandmother was dying – well, that would have made anybody depressed.'

Jill's grandmother spent most of her life in a small country town in the outback. She loved horses, open space, greenery, the wind and looking out at the vast blue sky. This is what she craved at the end of her life, but she couldn't have been further from that reality. Despite all the staff being incredibly friendly, warm and understanding, Jill said her grandmother was scared of being left alone in that big dark room. Despite Jill's reassurances, she said she could still see the scared look in her grandmother's eyes. Being afraid isn't a pleasant way to spend the last moments of one's life.

Reflecting on Jill's experience now, I can't help but think that to give her grandmother the opportunity to experience the outback again, through virtual reality, would have been calming and grounding for her. I imagine having something else to look at would have been a very useful tonic at that time. It would have been something to talk, think and reminisce about – though still no substitute for being able to hold Jill's hand through to her last breaths.

There is emerging evidence indicating that providing terminal cancer patients with the opportunity to visit a memorable place or to return home with virtual reality headsets helps them. One study with 20 terminal cancer patients found that it significantly reduced pain, drowsiness, and depressive and anxious symptoms, while at the same time improving their wellbeing. The study also found there were no complaints.[7] Imagine how many people, from all walks of life – the elderly, children – could benefit from technology such as this. Understandably not all would want to, and more research needs to be done, but it could make a real difference to the quality of life at those final stages.

My colleague Dr Jamin Day is doing work at the moment using virtual reality to examine a compassionate mind training exercise called 'safe place imagery'. In this exercise, the aim is to imagine a place where you feel completely safe. A place where you have the feeling of being free to do anything you would like. This can be a real place or a completely new place you have created for yourself. In the exercise we try to connect to the sensory qualities of the place, so we ask, 'In this place you are creating for yourself, what do you see? Can you see the ocean, trees, a blue sky perhaps? What colours do you notice? Are they bright and rich or dark and earthy? Is it day or night? What is the temperature like? Is it cold? Warm? Maybe hot? Can you feel the wind against your skin? What noises can you hear? If you are outside can you hear birds or the leaves in the wind? Are there any smells, like the smell of the ocean, or flowers?' We really try to connect to the place with the senses.

We then pivot to creating a relationship with this place. So we ask you to imagine what it would feel like if this place welcomed you. If it was really happy to have you there. So if you are at the beach, the waves might say, 'It is good to see you' with warmth and friendliness. Or if you are sitting in the park, the trees might say, 'We are glad you are here with us.' In this exercise we are trying to create a sense of belonging, wanting and acceptance. Often our minds can be scary, especially when we don't know what memories might pop up. On top of that, many of us can feel very alone. This exercise deliberately creates a place in your mind that is yours, where you completely fit in and belong.

We then ask, 'In this place where you belong, what do you find yourself doing?' You might be lying back peacefully, or you might be running through the grass, or even kayaking through rapids. If you feel you can't do what you want to do, we'll suggest you change your place. It is your place, so you can create whatever you need.

Many patients love this exercise. I love this exercise. It can be a really calming, grounding and freeing experience. Some patients cry after they have done it because of the feeling of peace it affords.

Jamin is seeing whether this exercise has an even bigger impact in virtual reality. Does it have a stronger emotional hit? Do patients remember it more? Do they find it easier? Does it open their creative energies, allowing them to feel a real sense of connection? He is doing this using a technology called Tilt Brush. In Tilt Brush you are in a three-dimensional world, so as you are painting and creating your safe place, it gives the feeling that you are really there. Again, this might not be for everyone, but for some, especially those for whom imagery is difficult, transitioning the exercise to virtual reality might help create the safety and freedom that the exercise is meant to provide. Adding sensory elements, like sound, to Tilt Brush can also really help. Indeed, my friend and colleague Dr Stan Steindl is doing work with Dr Anthony Garcia to pair meditation with music, helping provide a greater sensory connection.

AI and digital technologies offer a sea of possibilities. Like progression into any new territory there will be mistakes along the way with how we develop, design and use it. We are already recognising some of these, such as the in-built biases that occur in the design process, that erode some of the confidence we may have had that such technologies would be purely objective. Will AI be the antidote to the world's problems when it comes to mental health and loneliness? I am not hopeful. I think people need people. However, for those who have been cruelly treated by humans, building trusting relationships with AI or carebots might be the first step in developing relationships with others.

I do think AI and digital technologies can be complementary to human contact, rather than replacing it entirely. Consider a couple who are now in their late 80s. They have lived a life where they have loved and cared for each other, seen each other – and their children and grandchildren – grow and flourish. Now one of the partners is unwell and requires significant care. In these instances I think AI-driven carebots can help maintain the dignity and intimacy of the relationship, without the ill partner feeling like a 'burden', or worse yet, a 'child'. Spouses who become carers have to bathe, dress and feed their partners, as well as assist with toileting. Doing these tasks can diminish the sense of intimacy and equality in a relationship. The loss of function is compounded with the further loss of the original form of the relationship.

There is a large body of research that demonstrates that those caring for their partner in later stages of life see themselves, their partner and the relationship in a significantly altered way.[8] According to the World Health Organization, right now around the world there are estimated to be about 55 million-plus people living with dementia, and many of these people require high levels of care.[9] Most of that care comes from family caregivers, and the largest proportion of care is given by spouses. Critically, caring for a spouse isn't all negative. Many carers experience positives, such as increased togetherness, strengthened bonds and feelings of accomplishment. Indeed, some will reflect on how in their vows they said 'in sickness and in health'. Part of what gives life and the relationship meaning is doing these things. Despite that, I think at least the option of AI carebots for those who find themselves in a situation where they are providing caregiving provides more good than harm.

If we make compassion central to how we use these technologies, we might not be able to stop suffering completely, but there is great hope that we will be able to reduce the severity and frequency of suffering on large scales.

Epilogue

The next time you are out on a morning walk you might not see a drowning child, but you might see a person who is homeless. If you do, will you decide to stop and help? The aim of this book is not to make you feel guilty or embarrassed about your lack of immediate compassionate action every time you observe suffering, but rather to help you reflect on how you make your decisions to act compassionately. Are there certain groups or causes you gravitate to more easily than others? What do you tell yourself so you don't feel guilty about not helping all the time?

My colleagues and I looked at the relationship between guilt and prosocial actions in a study.[1] We looked at acts such as consoling someone in distress, and asked, 'To what extent would you feel guilty if you didn't do these prosocial acts?' Participants had to respond on a scale from 1 (not at all) to 9 (very much). Data from over 300 participants indicated that people would feel moderately guilty if they didn't do the prosocial act, with an average score of 6.15 out of 9. We were also interested in whether participants felt *resentful* about the expectation they should help others, but scores here were low, with an average of 3.47 out of 9. Finally, we asked, 'Do you feel there is too big an expectation to help others?' Again, the score was low, with an average of 3.86 out of 9. What can we conclude from this? At our core we like to help and feel guilty if we don't, and we like to live in societies that value helping.

These sentiments have been echoed around the globe during COVID-19. We have made sacrifices and done, with repetitive boredom, a number of small to large prosocial acts. We might not have experienced joy doing these acts, but they were meaningful because we care about helping others. Sure there were some notable exceptions, where some people deliberately and falsely made claims that jeopardised the health of others, but overwhelmingly we did the right thing.

Despite the hundreds if not thousands of studies that have been conducted showing compassion is helpful for us, we still don't always decide to act compassionately. Sometimes we're too busy, or it's too difficult, too costly, not our problem. We might not even notice suffering at all. It's maddening. Right now, humanity is being confronted with some stark realities that will cause immense suffering unless we start to take compassionate action. Climate change and COVID-19 aren't going to leave us anytime soon; there are microplastics found everywhere on Earth, from the top of Mt Everest to the bottom of our sea floors; and as you read this book, an estimated 264 million people have depression. Just like taxes, suffering is a fact of life. And so must compassion be, too.

I hope what is heartening here is a sense of recognition that we do see compassion everywhere. We are an incredibly compassionate species. Even though we rarely hear the word 'compassion' uttered by our politicians or our journalists. When Barack Obama famously said we need empathy more than ever, I was hopeful we would see a rush of compassion at the heart of our political leadership. But compassion for the most part seems to remain in the dark. Even in the midst of the horrors of COVID-19, little has been said about compassion. Rather, we hear terms like 'restrictions' and 'social distancing', which create a feeling of threat and punishment. Using the right language to talk about the actions we can take to support each other and reduce suffering is very important. We could use terms like 'safe relating' instead of 'social distancing'. Even 'physical distancing' is better. Or we could use terms like 'protections' instead of 'restrictions'. How we frame things matters.

What we choose to believe also matters. Gene Roddenberry, the creator of *Star Trek*, was far too generous towards humans. In his future world, the 23rd century, humans no longer selfishly pursue greed, as all our basic necessities for money, energy, education and housing are met. We are free instead to spend our time on higher callings, like art, exploration and the pursuit of knowledge. In contrast, one life form, the Ferengi, are a civilisation built on free enterprise, where money and profit are the sole goals of life. When I see our lack of urgency on issues such as homelessness, poverty, hunger and climate change I can't help but feel we have no hope of reaching the level of advancement depicted in *Star Trek*. Rather, we are doomed to be like the Ferengi forever. But choosing to believe that has consequences. It means I see actions through a specific lens, one that is selfish and greedy and not particularly compassionate.

Dr Jamil Zaki did a very clever study with his graduate student Dr Erika Weisz, where they asked undergraduate students to write to high school students about empathy.[2] One group of undergrads had to write letters that conveyed that empathy is a fixed entity, something you have or don't. The other group were instructed to depict empathy as something that you can grow. Like a muscle, it just requires some training. The idea was that reading these letters might help the high school students build friendships. Unbeknown to the undergraduate students, however, Jamil and Erika were really interested in whether writing a letter about empathy as fixed or dynamic influenced the way they themselves experienced empathy. Put another way, would the students begin to believe the messages they were writing? To my surprise, they did. Those students who wrote about empathy as fixed had no changes in their empathy levels, but those who wrote about it being something you can develop had significant growth in their own levels of empathy two months later. This is such a clever and low-cost study, not requiring weeks of meditation.

So I choose to believe we are capable of realising the human dream portrayed by *Star Trek*. And when I look through that lens, I see the extraordinary things humans have done and continue to do. The millions who volunteer, donate and sacrifice their time and even their lives to help others. Across the course of our history, despite all the changes that have occurred in how we live, the medical advancements we have made, and the new technologies that have been built, one bright star that has always remained constant is that humanity has striven to show compassion for each other. There are times this has wavered – we aren't perfect – but there have always been those willing to show immense courage to correct our course and advance the cause of compassion.

There is much still to do, and there are times when things seem dire, but we just need to open our eyes and look to see how many people around the world are trying to think, feel and act compassionately. It's inspiring.

Acknowledgements

Over two years ago, I received an email from UQP Publishing Director Madonna Duffy asking if I had ever considered writing a book. I must confess, it was not on my radar. But at our first meeting, Madonna lit my enthusiasm.

A few weeks later the whole world changed. COVID-19 was upon us.

Since that moment, it has felt like I have been writing a book on compassion in a constant sea of tragedy. There were days I just didn't want to write about compassion. But I have been lucky; Madonna Duffy and Margot Lloyd from UQP have been the most supportive editors I could have asked for. I am extremely grateful for their ideas, reassurances and support. I am a first-time writer and there were many times

I felt completely out of my depth, yet they always found the positives in what I was doing and made me feel confident. I suspect that is a hard skill to get right, and I deeply appreciate that expertise. Thank you.

The client stories discussed in this book are totally de-identified and a combination of different cases. I am grateful for the opportunity to be a psychologist and am amazed at the courage of my patients.

Before I list all the amazing people who helped me along the way I have to single out Paul Gilbert. He totally changed my research direction and helped shape me as a researcher and a clinician. I am deeply indebted to him and am constantly in awe of both his generosity and intelligence.

I want to thank James Doty, who hosted me as a Fellow at Stanford CCARE. I remain forever grateful for his continued support. I also had a lot of help from the scientific community, with colleagues willing to read chapters, provide feedback on my ideas and answer my emails. I hope I haven't missed anyone, but thank you Matti Wilks, Stan Steindl, Nicola Petrocchi, Marcela Matos, Alasdair Foster, David Cowan, James Bennett-Levy, Kelly Kirkland and Jamin Day. Members of my lab have also been extremely helpful in providing ideas and reading drafts. Thank you to Chase Sherwell, Deanna Varley, Dylan Moloney-Gibb, Jeffrey Kim, Alicia Carter and April Hoang. I must also thank my friends, who showed a real enthusiasm towards my book, despite it not being about something more exciting. Thanks Brendan, Jerome, Duncan, James, James, Jamie and Minh. Funnily, our running competition was very useful for me, as I found when I went running fresh new ideas would pop into my head about the book. I ran so much because I found it so helpful for writing that I ended up winning a few of our monthly competitions for time spent exercising.

I also had incredible support at home. Thank you to my mum and dad, as well as Catherine, Thomas and William, for putting up with my thoughts and complaints regarding writing about compassion. And thank you also to my mother-in-law, Dell, my father-in-law, Dick, and my brother-in-law, Scott, for your helpful feedback, humour and support. My family were always the first to read my drafts. I'd email a chapter to them and within an hour I would have text message responses with words of encouragement. That meant a great deal to me.

To Fletcher and Sofia, never could I believe that two such small humans could radiate such warmth, love and joy. I know you are both disappointed I didn't write 'poo poo bum bum', but one day you will understand why.

Finally, the biggest thank you is for my wife, Cassie Tellegen. Without her this book wouldn't have been written. Cassie, you listened to me for countless hours while I tried to explain my clumsy ideas and you helped shape them into more coherent stories. There were many times I was down about things with the book, and every time you were there, my ideal compassionate other. I wrote this book under the stairs of our house and during these last few difficult years when we have all been living on top of each other during lockdowns, you managed to keep Fletcher and Sofia entertained for long stretches so I could write. I owe you big time and love you so much.

Notes

PROLOGUE

1   Inzlicht, M, Shenhav, A & Olivola, CY (2018). 'The Effort Paradox: Effort is both costly and valued'. *Trends in Cognitive Sciences*, vol. 22, no. 4, pp. 337–349.

CHAPTER 1: WHAT IS COMPASSION?

1   Gilbert, P (2014). 'The Origins and Nature of Compassion Focused Therapy'. *British Journal of Clinical Psychology*, vol. 53, pp. 6–41.

2   Zaki, J (2021). *The War for Kindness: Building empathy in a fractured world*, Little, Brown, London.

3   Atkins, PWB, Wilson, DS & Hayes, SC (2019). *Prosocial: Using evolutionary science to build productive, equitable, and collaborative groups*. Context Press, Oakland.

4   Coan, JA, Schaefer, HS & Davidson, RJ (2006). 'Lending a Hand: Social regulation of the neural response to threat'. *Psychological Science*, 17, pp. 1032–1039.

5   Trzeciak, S & Mazzarelli, A (2019). *Compassionomics: The revolutionary*

scientific evidence that caring makes a difference, Studer Group, Pensacola.

6   Goetz, JL, Keltner, D & Simon-Thomas, E (2010). 'Compassion: An evolutionary analysis and empirical review'. *Psychological Bulletin*, vol. 136, no. 3, pp. 351–374.

7   Bloom, P (2016). *Against Empathy: The case for rational compassion*, HarperCollins Publishers, New York.

8   Heinz K (1981, 2010). 'On Empathy'. *International Journal of Psychoanalytic Self Psychology*, vol. 5, no. 2, pp. 122–131.

9   Batson, CD, Klein, TR, Highberger, L & Shaw, LL (1995). 'Immorality from Empathy-Induced Altruism: When compassion and justice conflict'. *Journal of Personality and Social Psychology*, vol. 68, no. 6, pp. 1042–1054.

10   Australian Red Cross (2020). *9 out of 10 Australians Think We Should Be More Kind Every Day*, media release, accessed online.

11   Bloom, P (2017). 'Empathy and Its Discontents'. *Trends in Cognitive Sciences*, vol. 21, pp. 24–31.

12   Hein, G, Silani, G, Preuschoff, K, Batson, CD & Singer, T (2010). 'Neural Responses to Ingroup and Outgroup Members' Suffering Predict Individual Differences in Costly Helping'. *Neuron*, vol. 68, pp. 149–160.

13   Darley, JM & Batson, CD (1973). '"From Jerusalem to Jericho": A study of situational and dispositional variables in helping behavior'. *Journal of Personality and Social Psychology*, vol. 27, no. 1, pp. 100–108.

14   See more at their website, effectivealtruism.org.au.

15   Ord, T (2013). 'The Moral Imperative toward Cost-Effectiveness in Global Health'. *Center for Global Development*, accessed online.

16   Worline, MC & Dutton, JE (2017). *Awakening Compassion at Work: The quiet power that elevates people and organizations*, Berrett-Koehler, Oakland.

17   Batson, CD, O'Quin, K, Fultz, J, Vanderplas, M & Isen, AM (1983). 'Influence of Self-Reported Distress and Empathy on Egoistic Versus Altruistic Motivation to Help'. *Journal of Personality and Social Psychology*, vol. 45, no. 3, pp. 706–718.

18   Fowler, JH & Christakis, NA (2010). 'Cooperative Behavior Cascades in Human Social Networks'. *Proceedings of the National Academy of Sciences of the United States of America*, vol. 107, no. 12, pp. 5334–5338.

19   Condon, P & DeSteno, D (2011). 'Compassion for One Reduces Punishment for Another'. *Journal of Experimental Social Psychology*, vol. 47, pp. 698–701.

20 Gilbert, P, Basran, J, MacArthur, M & Kirby, JN (2019). 'Differences in the Semantics of Prosocial Words: An exploration of compassion and kindness'. *Mindfulness*, vol. 10, no. 11, pp. 2259–2271.

CHAPTER 2: THE THINGS THAT MOVE US

1 Volunteering Australia (2017). 'Giving Australia 2016: Fact sheet – individual volunteering', *VolunteeringAustralia.org*, accessed online.

2 Charities Aid Foundation (2019). 'CAF World Giving Index Tenth Edition: Ten years of giving trends', *CAFonline.org*, accessed online.

3 Marsh, AA, Stoycos, SA, Brethel-Haurwitz, KM, Robinson, P, VanMeter, JW & Cardinale EM (2014). 'Neural and Cognitive Characteristics of Extraordinary Altruists'. *Proceedings of the National Academy of Sciences*, vol. 111, no. 42, pp. 15036–15041.

4 Johnston, WM & Davey, GCL (1997). 'The Psychological Impact of Negative TV News Bulletins: The catastrophizing of personal worries'. *British Journal of Psychology*, vol. 88, pp. 85–91.

5 Philpot, R, Liebst, LS, Levine, M, Bernasco, W & Lindegaard, MR (2020). 'Would I Be Helped? Cross-national CCTV footage shows that intervention is the norm in public conflicts'. *American Psychologist*, vol. 75, no. 1, pp. 66–75.

6 Burger, JM (2009). 'Replicating Milgram: Would people still obey today?'. *American Psychologist*, vol. 64, no. 1, pp. 1–11.

7 Haslam SA & Reicher SD (2012). 'Contesting the "Nature" of Conformity: What Milgram and Zimbardo's studies really show'. *PLoS Biology*, vol. 10, no. 11.

8 Haslam, SA, Reicher, SD, & Van Bavel, JJ (2019). 'Rethinking the Nature of Cruelty: The role of identity leadership in the Stanford Prison Experiment'. *American Psychologist*, vol. 74, no. 7, pp. 809–822.

9 Reicher, S & Haslam, SA (2006). 'Rethinkng the Psychology of Tyranny: The BBC prison study'. *British Journal of Social Psychology*, vol. 45, pp. 1–40.

10 Gilbert, P (2020). 'Compassion: From its evolution to a psychotherapy'. *Frontiers in Psychology*, vol. 11.

11 Ekers D, Webster L, Van Straten A, Cuijpers P, Richards D & Gilbody S (2014). 'Behavioural Activation for Depression: An update of meta-analysis of effectiveness and sub group analysis. *PLoS One,* vol. 9, no. 6.

12   Adie, T, Steindl, SR, Kirby, JN, Kane, RT & Mazzucchelli TG (2021). 'The Relationship Between Self-Compassion and Depressive Symptoms: Avoidance and activation as mediators'. *Mindfulness*, vol. 12, no. 7, pp. 1748–1756.

13   Mitchell, AE, Whittingham, K, Steindl, S & Kirby J (2018). 'Feasibility and Acceptability of a Brief Online Self-Compassion Intervention for Mothers of Infants'. *Archives of Women's Mental Health*, vol. 21, no. 5, pp. 553–561; Lennard, GR, Mitchell, AE & Whittingham, K (2021). 'Randomized Controlled Trial of a Brief Online Self-Compassion Intervention for Mothers of Infants: Effects on mental health outcomes'. *Journal of Clinical Psychology*, vol. 77, no. 3, pp 473–487.

14   Dunbar, RIM (2009). 'The Social Brain Hypothesis and Its Implications for Social Evolution'. *Annals of Human Biology*, vol. 36, no. 5, pp. 562–572.

15   Zaki, J (2020). 'Catastrophe Compassion: Understanding and extending prosociality under crisis'. *Trends in Cognitive Sciences*, vol. 24, no. 8, pp. 587–589.

16   Gilbert, P, Basran, J, MacArthur, M & Kirby, JN. 'Differences in the Semantics of Prosocial Words'.

17   Zaki, J. *The War for Kindness*.

CHAPTER 3: THINKING OUR WAY TO COMPASSION

1   Suddendorf, T & Corballis, MC (2007). 'The Evolution of Foresight: What is mental time travel, and is it unique to humans?'. *The Behavioral and Brain Sciences*, vol. 30, no. 3, pp. 299–351.

2   Redshaw, J & Suddendorf, T (2020). 'Temporal Junctures in the Mind'. *Trends in Cognitive Sciences*, vol. 24, no.1, pp. 52–64.

3   Redshaw, J & Suddendorf, T (2016). 'Children's and Apes' Preparatory Responses to Two Mutually Exclusive Possibilities'. *Current Biology*, vol. 26, no. 13, pp. 1758–1762.

4   ibid.

5   Laham, SM (2009). 'Expanding the Moral Circle: Inclusion and exclusion mindsets and the circle of moral ground'. *Journal of Experimental Social Psychology*, vol. 45, pp. 250–253.

6   Chapman, CM, Masser, BM & Louis, WR (2020). 'Identity Motives in Charitable Giving: Explanations for charity preferences from a global donor survey'. *Psychology & Marketing*, vol. 37, no. 9, pp. 1277– 1291.

7 Arnocky, S, Piché, T, Albert, G, Ouellette, D & Barclay, P (2017). 'Altruism Predicts Mating Success in Humans'. *The British Journal of Psychology*, vol. 108, no. 2, pp. 416–435.

8 Spikins, P (2015). *How Compassion Made Us Human: An archaeology of Stone Age sentiment*, Pen and Sword Archaeology, Barnsley.

CHAPTER 4: COMPASSION IN THE FAMILY

1 Hintsanen, M, Gluschkoff, K, Dobewall, H, Cloninger, CR, Keltner, D, Saarinen, A, Wesolowska, K, Volanen, SM, Raitakari, OT & Pulkki-Råback, L (2019). 'Parent-Child-Relationship Quality Predicts Offspring Dispositional Compassion in Adulthood: A prospective follow-up study over three decades'. *Developmental Psychology*, vol. 55, no. 1, pp. 216–225.

2 Kirby, JN (2019). 'Nurturing Family Environments for Children: Compassion-focused parenting as a form of parenting intervention'. *Education Sciences*, vol. 10, no. 1, p. 3.

3 Kirby, JN, Sampson, H, Day, J, Hayes, A & Gilbert, P (2019). 'Human Evolution and Culture in Relationship to Shame in the Parenting Role: Implications for psychology and psychotherapy'. *Psychology and Psychotherapy*, vol. 92, no. 2, pp. 238–260.

4 Hrdy, SB (2011). *Mothers and Others: The evolutionary origins of mutual understanding*, Belknap Press, Cambridge.

5 ibid.

6 Australian Bureau of Statistics (2015). '4402.0 – Childhood Education and Care, Australia, June 2011', *ABS.gov.au*, accessed online.

7 Coall, DA & Hertwig, R (2010). 'Grandparental Investment: Past, present, and future'. *Behavioral and Brain Sciences*, vol. 33, no. 1, pp. 1–19.

8 Ahnert, L, Gunnar, MR, Lamb, ME & Barthel, M (2004). 'Transition to Child Care: Associations with infant–mother attachment, infant negative emotion, and cortisol elevations'. *Child Development*, vol. 75, no. 3, pp. 639–650.

9 Lisonbee, JA, Mize, J, Payne, AL & Granger, DA (2008). 'Children's Cortisol and the Quality of Teacher–Child Relationships in Child Care'. *Child Development*, vol. 79, no. 6, pp. 1818–1832.

10 Eibl-Eibesfeldt, I (1989). *Human Ethology*, Routledge, New York.

11 Montagu, A (1971). *Touching: The human significance of the skin*, Columbia University Press, New York.

12 Campbell-Yeo, ML, Disher, TC, Benoit, BL & Johnston, CC (2015). 'Understanding Kangaroo Care and Its Benefits to Preterm Infants'. *Pediatric Health, Medicine and Therapeutics*, vol. 6, pp. 15–32.

13 Beutel, ME, Klein, EM, Brähler, E, Reiner, I, Jünger, C, Michal M, Wiltink, J, Wild, PS, Münzel, T, Lackner, KJ & Tibubos, AN (2017). 'Loneliness in the General Population: Prevalence, determinants and relations to mental health'. *BMC Psychiatry*, vol. 17, no. 1, p. 97.

14 Cacioppo, S, Capitanio, JP & Cacioppo, JT (2014). 'Toward a Neurology of Loneliness'. *Psychological Bulletin*, vol. 140, no. 6, pp. 1464–1504.

15 Buettner, D, Nelson, T & Veenhoven, R (2020). 'Ways to Greater Happiness: A Delphi study'. *Journal of Happiness Studies*, vol. 21, pp. 2789–2806.

16 Chiu, M, Rahman, F, Vigod, S, Lau, C, Cairney, J & Kurdyak, P (2018). 'Mortality in Single Fathers Compared with Single Mothers and Partnered Parents: A population-based cohort study'. *The Lancet Public Health*, vol. 3, no. 3, pp e115–e123.

17 Damaske, S, Bratter, JL & Frech, A (2017). 'Single Mother Families and Employment, Race, and Poverty in Changing Economic Times'. *Social Science Research*, vol. 62, pp. 120–133.

18 Seltzer, LJ, Prososki, AR, Ziegler, TE & Pollak, SD (2012). 'Instant Messages Vs. Speech: Hormones and why we still need to hear each other'. *Evolution and Human Behavior*, vol. 33, no. 1, pp. 42–45.

19 Li, NP, van Vugt, M & Colarelli, SM (2017). 'The Evolutionary Mismatch Hypothesis: Implications for psychological science'. *Current Directions in Psychological Science*, vol. 27, no. 1, pp. 38–44.

20 Rolfe, H (2005). *Men in Childcare*, Working Paper Series no. 35, Equal Opportunities Commission, Manchester.

21 ZERO TO THREE (2016). *National Parent Survey Report*, ZERO TO THREE, Washington, accessed online.

22 Cassidy, J, Jones, JD & Shaver, PR (2013). 'Contributions of Attachment Theory and Research: A framework for future research, translation, and policy'. *Development and Psychopathology*, vol. 25, no. 4, pp. 1415–1434.

23 Yoshida, S & Funato, H (2021). 'Physical Contact in Parent–Infant Relationship and Its Effect on Fostering a Feeling of Safety'. *iScience*, vol. 24, no. 7, p. 102721.

24 Clay, Z & de Waal, FBM (2013). 'Development of Socio-Emotional Competence in Bonobos'. *PNAS*, vol. 110, no. 45, pp. 18121–18126.

25 Mackes, NK, Golm, D, Sarkar, S, Kumsta, R, Rutter, M, Fairchild, G, Mehta, MA & Sonuga-Barke, EJS (2020). 'Early Childhood Deprivation Is Associated with Alterations in Adult Brain Structure Despite Subsequent Environmental Enrichment'. *PNAS*, vol. 117, no. 1, pp. 641–649.

26 Sanders, MR, Markie-Dadds, C, Rinaldis, M, Firman, D & Baig, N (2007). 'Using Household Survey Data to Inform Policy Decisions Regarding the Delivery of Evidence-Based Parenting Interventions'. *Child: Care, health and development*, vol. 33, no. 6, pp. 768–783.

27 Gershoff, ET & Grogan-Kaylor, A (2016). 'Spanking and Child Outcomes: Old controversies and new meta-analyses'. *Journal of Family Psychology*, vol. 30, no. 4, pp. 453–469.

28 Miller, JG, Kahle, S, Lopez, M & Hastings, PD (2015). 'Compassionate Love Buffers Stress-Reactive Mothers from Fight-or-Flight Parenting'. *Developmental Psychology*, vol. 51, no. 1, pp. 36–43.

29 Hoang, N-PT, Kirby, JN, Haslam, DM & Sanders, MR (2022). 'Promoting Positive Relationship between Parents and Grandparents: A randomized controlled trial of group Triple P Plus compassion in Vietnam'. *Behavior Therapy*, in press.

30 Miller, JG, Kahle, S, Troxel, NR & Hastings, PD (2020). 'The Development of Generosity from Four to Six Years: Examining stability and the biopsychosocial contributions of children's vagal flexibility and mothers' compassion'. *Frontiers in Psychology*, vol. 11.

31 Poehlmann-Tynan, J, Engbretson, A, Vigna, AB, Weymouth, LA, Burnson, C, Zahn-Waxler, C, Kapoor, A, Gerstein, ED, Fanning, KA & Raison, CL (2020). 'Cognitively-Based Compassion Training for Parents Reduces Cortisol in Infants and Young Children'. *Infant Mental Health Journal*, vol. 41, no. 1, pp. 126–144.

32 Hoang, N-PT, Kirby, JN, Haslam, DM & Sanders, MR. 'Promoting Positive Relationship between Parents and Grandparents'.

33 Weinberg, MK, Beeghly, M, Olson, KL & Tronick, E (2008). 'A Still-Face Paradigm for Young Children: two-and-a-half-year-olds' reactions to maternal unavailability during the still-face. *The Journal of Developmental Processes*, vol. 3, no. 1, pp. 4–22.

34 For a review, see Harvard's Centre on the Developing Child website.

35 Suizzo, MA (2007). 'Parents' Goals and Values for Children: Dimensions of independence and interdependence across four US ethnic groups'. *Journal of Cross-Cultural Psychology*, vol. 38, no. 4, pp. 506–530.

36 Bluth, K, Roberson, PNE, Gaylord, SA, Faurot, KR, Grewen, KM, Arzon, S & Girdler, SS (2016). 'Does Self-Compassion Protect Adolescents from Stress?'. *Journal of Child and Family Studies*, vol. 25, no. 4, pp. 1098–1109.

37 Bluth, K & Eisenlohr-Moul, TA (2017). 'Response to a Mindful Self-Compassion Intervention in Teens: A within-person association of mindfulness, self-compassion, and emotional well-being outcomes'. *Journal of Adolescence*, vol. 57, pp. 108–118.

CHAPTER 5: FEARS OF COMPASSION

1 Gilbert, P & Procter, S (2006). 'Compassionate Mind Training for People with High Shame and Self-Criticism: Overview and pilot study of a group therapy approach'. *Clinical Psychology and Psychotherapy*, vol. 13, no. 6, pp. 353–379.

2 Matos, M, Duarte, J & Pinto-Gouveia, J (2017). 'The Origins of Fears of Compassion: Shame and lack of safeness memories, fears of compassion and psychopathology'. *The Journal of Psychology*, vol. 151, no. 8, pp. 804–819.

3 Slepian, ML, Kirby, JN & Kalokerinos, EK (2020). 'Shame, Guilt, and Secrets on the Mind'. *Emotion*, vol. 20, no. 2, pp. 323–328.

4 Slepian ML & Kirby JN (2018). 'To Whom Do We Confide Our Secrets?'. *Personality and Social Psychology Bulletin*, vol. 44, no. 7, pp. 1008–1023.

5 Steindl, SR, Matos, M & Creed, AK (2021). 'Early Shame and Safeness Memories, and Later Depressive Symptoms and Safe Affect: The mediating role of self-compassion'. *Current Psychology*, vol. 40, no. 2, pp. 761–771.

6 Kirby, JN, Day, J & Sagar, V (2019). 'The "Flow" of Compassion: A meta-analysis of the fears of compassion scales and psychological functioning'. *Clinical Psychology Review*, vol. 70, pp. 26–39.

CHAPTER 6: TRAINING COMPASSION

1 Oscarsson, M, Carlbring, P, Andersson, G & Rozental, A (2020). 'A Large-Scale Experiment on New Year's Resolutions: Approach-oriented goals are more successful than avoidance-oriented goals'. *PLoS One*, vol. 15, no. 12.

2 Galante, J, Galante, I, Bekkers, M-J & Gallacher, J (2014). 'Effect of

Kindness-Based Meditation on Health and Well-Being: A systematic review and meta-analysis'. *Journal of Consulting and Clinical Psychology*, vol. 82, no. 6, pp. 1101–1114.

3   Hofmann, SG, Grossman, P & Hinton, DE (2011). 'Loving-Kindness and Compassion Meditation: Potential for psychological interventions'. *Clinical Psychology Review*, vol. 31, no. 7, pp. 1126–1132.

4   Jazaieri, H, Jinpa, GT, McGonigal, K, Rosenberg, EL, Finkelstein, J, Simon-Thomas, E, Cullen, M, Doty, JR, Gross, JJ & Goldin, PR (2012). 'Enhancing Compassion: A randomized controlled trial of a compassion cultivation training program'. *Journal of Happiness Studies*, vol. 14, no. 4, pp. 1113–1126.

5   Killingsworth, MA & Gilbert, DT (2010). 'A Wandering Mind Is an Unhappy Mind'. *Science*, vol. 330, no. 6006, p. 932.

6   Kirby, JN, Tellegen, CL & Steindl, SR (2017). 'A Meta-Analysis of Compassion-Based Interventions: Current state of knowledge and future directions'. *Behavior Therapy*, vol. 48, no. 6, pp. 778–792.

7   Reddan, MC, Wager, TD & Sciller, D (2018). 'Attenuating Neural Threat Expression with Imagination'. *Neuron*, vol. 100, no. 4, pp. 994–1005.

8   Condon, P, Desbordes, G, Miller, WB & DeSteno, D (2013). 'Meditation Increases Compassionate Responses to Suffering'. *Psychological Science*, vol. 24, no. 10, pp. 2125–2127.

9   Fogg, BJ (2019). *Tiny Habits: The small changes that change everything*, Ebury Publishing, London.

CHAPTER 7: THE DIFFICULTIES OF SELF-COMPASSION

1   Condon, P & Makransky, J (2020). 'Recovering the Relational Starting Point of Compassion Training: A foundation for sustainable and inclusive care'. *Perspectives on Psychological Science*, vol. 15, no. 6, pp. 1346–1362.

2   Kim, JJ, Kent, KM, Cunnington, R, Gilbert, P & Kirby JN (2020). 'Attachment Styles Modulate Neural Markers of Threat and Imagery When Engaging in Self-Criticism'. *Scientific Reports*, vol. 10, no. 1.

3   Kim, JJ, Parker, SL, Doty, JR, Cunnington, R, Gilbert, P & Kirby JN (2020). 'Neurophysiological and Behavioural Markers of Compassion'. *Scientific Reports*, vol. 10, no. 1.

4   Werner, AM, Tibubos, AN, Rohrmann, S & Reiss, N (2019). 'The Clinical Trait Self-Criticism and Its Relation to Psychopathology:

A systematic review – update'. *Journal of Affective Disorders*, vol. 246, pp. 530–547.

5   Gilbert, P. 'Compassion'.

6   Jazaieri, H, Jinpa, GT, McGonigal, K, Rosenberg, EL, Finkelstein, J, Simon-Thomas, E, Cullen, M, Doty, JR, Gross, JJ & Goldin PR. 'Enhancing Compassion'.

7   Matos, M, Duarte, J, Duarte, C, Gilbert, P & Pinto-Gouveia, J (2018). 'How One Experiences and Embodies Compassionate Mind Training Influences Its Effectiveness'. *Mindfulness*, vol. 9, pp. 1224–1235.

8   Keng, S-L, Smoski, MJ & Robins, CJ (2011). 'Effects of Mindfulness on Psychological Health: A review of empirical studies'. *Clinical Psychology Review*, vol. 31, no. 6, pp. 1041–1056.

9   Matos, M, Duarte, J, Duarte, C, Gilbert, P & Pinto-Gouveia, J. 'How One Experiences and Embodies Compassionate Mind Training Influences Its Effectiveness'.

10   Nesse, RM (2019). *Good Reasons for Bad Feelings: Insights from the frontier of evolutionary psychiatry*, Dutton, New York.

11   Gerritsen, RJS & Band, GPH (2018). 'Breath of Life: The respiratory vagal stimulation model of contemplative activity'. *Frontiers in Human Neuroscience*, vol. 12.

12   Allcott, H, Braghieri, L, Eichmeyer, S & Gentzkow, M (2020). 'The Welfare Effects of Social Media'. *American Economic Review*, vol. 110, no. 3, pp. 629–676.

13   Bekalu, MA, McCloud, RF & Viswanath, K (2019). 'Association of Social Media Use with Social Well-Being, Positive Mental Health, and Self-Rated Health: Disentangling routine use from emotional connection to use'. *Health Education & Behavior*, vol. 46, no. 2, pp. 69S–80S.

14   León, I, Hernández, JA, Rodríguez, S & Vila, J (2008). 'When Head Is Tempered by Heart: Heart rate variability modulates perception of other-blame reducing anger'. *Motivation and Emotion*, vol. 33, no. 1, pp. 1–9.

15   Gilbert, P. 'Compassion'.

16   Porges, SW. 'Vagal Pathways'.

17   Thayer, JF & Lane, RD (2000). 'A Model of Neurovisceral Integration in Emotion Regulation and Dysregulation'. *Journal of Affective Disorders*, vol. 61, no.3, pp. 201–216.

18   Di Bello, M, Carnevali, L, Petrocchi, N, Thayer, JF, Gilbert, P & Ottaviani, C (2020). 'The Compassionate Vagus: A meta-analysis on the

connection between compassion and heart rate variability'. *Neuroscience and Biobehavioral Reviews*, vol. 116, pp. 21–30.

19   Costello, JF & Plass, C (2001). 'Methylation Matters'. *Journal of Medical Genetics*, vol. 38, no. 5, pp. 285–303.

20   Martin, EM & Fry, RC (2018). 'Environmental Influences on the Epigenome: Exposure-associated DNA methylation in human populations'. *Annual Review of Public Health*, vol. 39, pp. 309–333.

21   Mitchell, C, Schneper, LM, & Notterman, DA (2016). 'DNA Methylation, Early Life Environment, and Health Outcomes'. *Pediatric Research*, vol. 79, pp. 212–219.

22   Thompson, R & Zuroff, DC (1999). 'Dependency, Self-Criticism, and Mothers' Responses to Adolescent Sons' Autonomy and Competence'. *Journal of Youth and Adolescence*, vol. 28, pp. 365–384.

23   Neff, KD & McGehee, P (2010). 'Self-Compassion and Psychological Resilience among Adolescents and Young Adults'. *Self and Identity*, vol. 9, pp. 225–240.

24   Irons, C, Gilbert, P, Baldwin, MW, Baccus, JR & Palmer, M (2006). 'Parental Recall, Attachment Relating and Self-Attacking/Self-Reassurance: Their relationship with depression'. *British Journal of Clinical Psychology*, vol. 45, no. 3, pp. 297–308.

25   Kim, JJ, Parker, SL, Doty, JR, Cunnington, R, Gilbert, P & Kirby, JN. 'Neurophysiological and Behavioural Markers of Compassion'.

26   Suddendorf, T & Corballis, MC. 'The Evolution of Foresight'.

27   Robinson, K (2006). 'Do Schools Kill Creativity?' *TED.com*, accessed online.

28   Whelton, WJ & Greenberg, LS (2005). 'Emotion in Self-Criticism'. *Personality and Individual Differences*, vol. 38, no. 7, pp. 1583–1595.

29   Kim, JJ, Henderson, T, Best, T, Cunnington, R & Kirby, JN (2020). 'Neural and Self-Report Markers of Reassurance: A generalized additive modelling approach'. *Frontiers in Psychiatry*, vol. 11.

30   Baumeister, RF, Bratslavsky, E, Finkenauer, C & Vohs, KD (2001). 'Bad Is Stronger than Good'. *Review of General Psychology*, vol. 5, no. 4, pp. 323–370.

31   Hamlin, JK & Wynn, K (2011). 'Young Infants Prefer Prosocial to Antisocial Others'. *Cognitive Development*, vol. 26, no. 1, pp. 30–39.

32   Tierney, J & Baumeister, RF (2019). *The Power of Bad: How the negativity effect rules us and how we can rule it*, Penguin Books, New York.

CHAPTER 8: THE ANATOMY OF SUFFERING

1   Leighton, TD (2003). *Faces of Compassion: Classic bodhisattva archetypes and their modern expression*, Wisdom Publications, Somerville; Vessantara (1993). *Meeting the Buddhas: A guide to buddhas, bodhisattvas, and tantric deities*, Windhorse Publications, Glasgow.

2   Vessantara. *Meeting the Buddhas.*

3   Dalai Lama & Ekman, P (2008). *Emotional Awareness: Overcoming the obstacles to psychological balance and compassion*, Times Books, New York.

4   Khoo, E-L, Small, R, Cheng, W, Hatchard, T, Glynn, B, Rice, DB, Skidmore, B, Kenny, S, Hutton, B & Poulin, PA (2019). 'Comparative Evaluation of Group-Based Mindfulness-Based Stress Reduction and Cognitive Behavioural Therapy for the Treatment and Management of Chronic Pain: A systematic review and network meta-analysis'. *Evidence Based Mental Health*, vol. 22, no. 1, pp. 26–35; Khoury, B, Sharma, M, Rush, SE & Fournier, C (2015). 'Mindfulness-Based Stress Reduction for Healthy Individuals: A meta-analysis'. *Journal of Psychosomatic Research*, vol. 78, no. 6, pp. 519–528.

5   Gonda, J (1963). 'The Indian Mantra'. *Oriens*, vol. 16, pp. 244–297.

6   Champion, L, Economides, M & Chandler, C (2018). 'The Efficacy of a Brief App-Based Mindfulness Intervention on Psychosocial Outcomes in Healthy Adults: A pilot randomised controlled trial'. *PLoS One*, vol. 13, no. 12.

7   Van Dam, NT, van Vugt, MK, Vago, DR, Schmalzl, L, Saron, CD, Olendzki, A, Meissner, T, Lazar, SW, Kerr, CE, Gorchov, J, Fox, KCR, Field, BA, Britton, WB, Brefczynski-Lewis, JA & Meyer, DE (2018). 'Mind the Hype: A critical evaluation and prescriptive agenda for research on mindfulness and meditation'. *Perspectives on Psychological Science*, vol. 13, no. 1, pp. 36–61.

8   Mason, MF & Reinholtz, N (2015). 'Avenues Down Which a Self-Reminding Mind Can Wander'. *Motivation Science*, vol. 1, no. 1, pp. 1–21

9   Bastian, B, Jetten, J & Fasoli, F (2011). 'Cleansing the Soul by Hurting the Flesh: The guilt-reducing effect of pain'. *Psychological Science*, vol. 22, no. 3, pp. 334–335.

10   Breines, JG & Chen, S (2012). 'Self-Compassion Increases Self-Improvement Motivation'. *Personality and Social Psychology Bulletin*, vol. 38, no. 9, pp. 1133–1143.

11 Wilson, TD, Reinhard, DA, Westgate, EC, Gilbert, DT, Ellerbeck, N, Hahn, C, Brown, CL & Shaked, A (2014). 'Just Think: The challenges of the disengaged mind'. *Science*, vol. 345, no. 6192, pp. 75–77.

12 Inzlicht, M, Shenhav, A & Olivola, CY. 'The Effort Paradox'.

13 Lim, D & DeSteno, D (2020). 'Past Adversity Protects Against the Numeracy Bias in Compassion'. *Emotion*, vol. 20, no. 8, pp. 1344–1356.

14 Sensky, T (2010). 'Suffering'. *International Journal of Integrated Care*, vol. 10, no. 5, pp. 66–68.

15 Kaufman, SB & Feingold, J (2022). *Choose Growth: A workbook for transcending trauma, fear, and self-doubt*. TarcherPerigee, New York.

16 Roland, D (2020). *The Power of Suffering: Growing through life crises*, Simon & Schuster, East Roseville.

17 Feldman, C & Kuyken, W (2011). 'Compassion in the Landscape of Suffering'. *Contemporary Buddhism*, vol. 12, no. 1, pp. 143–155.

18 Green, M, Kirby, JN & Nielsen, M (2018). 'The Cost of Helping: An exploration of compassionate responding in children'. *British Journal of Developmental Psychology*, vol. 36, no. 4, pp. 673–678.

19 Kirby, JN, Wilks, M, Green, M, Tanjitpiyanond, P, Chowdhury, N, Kirkland, K & Nielsen, M (2021). 'Testing the Bounds of Compassion in Young Children'. Preliminary report.

20 Vekaria, K, Brethel-Haurwitz, KM, Cardinale, EM, Stoycos, SA & Marsh, AA (2017). 'Social Discounting and Distance Perceptions in Costly Altruism'. *Nature Human Behaviour*, vol. 1.

21 Kirby, JN, Hoang, A & Crimston, CR (2022). 'Compassionate Mind Training Can Increase Moral Expansiveness: A randomised controlled trial'. Manuscript under review.

CHAPTER 9: WHEN COMPASSION COLLAPSES

1 Slovic, P, Västfjäll, D, Erlandsson, A & Gregory, R (2017). 'Iconic Photographs and the Ebb and Flow of Empathic Response to Humanitarian Disasters'. *PNAS*, vol. 114, no. 4, pp. 640–644.

2 ibid.

3 Tønnessen, M, Aradhya, S & Mussino, E (2021). 'How Assad Changed Population Growth in Sweden and Norway: Syrian refugees' impact on Nordic national and municipal demography'. *PLoS One*, vol. 16, no. 1.

4 Save the Children (2020). *2019 Annual Report*, accessed online.

5 Gilbert (personal communication, 2018).

6   Västfjäll, D, Slovic, P, Mayorga, M & Peters, E (2014). 'Compassion Fade: Affect and charity are greatest for a single child in need'. *PLoS One*, vol. 9, no. 6.

7   Small, DA, Loewenstein, G & Slovic, P (2007). 'Sympathy and Callousness: The impact of deliberative thought on donations to identifiable and statistical victims'. *Organizational Behavior and Human Decision Processes*, vol. 102, no. 2, pp. 143–153.

8   Cameron, CD & Payne, BK (2011). 'Escaping Affect: How motivated emotion regulation creates insensitivity to mass suffering'. *Journal of Personality and Social Psychology*, vol. 100, no. 1, pp. 1–15.

9   Dowling, T (2018). 'Compassion Does Not Fatigue!'. *The Canadian Veterinary Journal*, vol. 59, no. 7, pp. 749–750; Klimecki, O & Singer, T (2011). 'Empathic Distress Fatigue Rather Than Compassion Fatigue? Integrating findings from empathy research in psychology and social neuroscience', in Oakley, B, Knafo, A, Madhavan, G & Wilson, DS (eds.), *Pathological Altruism*. Oxford University Press, New York, pp. 368–383; Fernando, AT & Consedine, NS (2014). 'Beyond Compassion Fatigue: The transactional model of physician compassion'. *Journal of Pain and Symptom Management*, vol. 48, no. 2, pp. 289–298.

10   Gilbert, P. 'Compassion'; Dev, V, Fernando, AT, Lim, AG & Consedine, NS (2018). 'Does Self-Compassion Mitigate the Relationship between Burnout and Barriers to Compassion? A cross-sectional quantitative study of 799 nurses'. *International Journal of Nursing Studies*, vol. 81, pp. 81–88.

11   Crawford, P, Gilbert, P, Gilbert, J, Gale, C & Harvey, K (2013). 'The Language of Compassion in Acute Mental Health Care'. *Qualitative Health Research*, vol. 23, no. 6, pp. 719–727.

12   ibid.

13   Trzeciak, S & Mazzarelli, A. *Compassionomics.*

14   Olson, LL (2018). 'Building Compassionate Work Environments: The concept of and measurement of ethical climate'in Ulrich, CM & Grady, C (eds), *Moral Distress in the Health Professions*, Springer, Cham, pp. 95–101; Lilius, JM, Worline, MC, Maitlis, S, Kanov, J, Dutton, JE & Frost, P (2008). 'The Contours and Consequences of Compassion at Work'. *Journal of Organizational Behavior*, vol. 29, no. 2, pp. 193–218.

15   Maratos, FA, Gilbert, P & Gilbert, T (2019). 'Improving Well-Being in Higher Education: Adopting a compassionate approach', in Gibbs,

P, Jameson, J & Elwick, A (eds.), *Values of the University in a Time of Uncertainty*, Springer, Cham.

16 Slovic, P, Västfjäll, D, Erlandsson, A & Gregory, R. 'Iconic Photographs and the Ebb and Flow of Empathic Response to Humanitarian Disasters'.

CHAPTER 10: COMPASSIONATE CONTRADICTIONS

1 Davies, R (2016). 'Savage Budget Cuts Pull Australia Down in Foreign Aid Rankings'. *The Conversation*, accessed online.

2 Oliver, A (2017). 'The Lowy Institute Poll 2017: Understanding Australian attitudes to the world', *The Lowy Institute*, accessed online.

3 López, A, Sanderman, R, Ranchor, AV & Schroevers, MJ (2018). 'Compassion for Others and Self-Compassion: Levels, correlates, and relationship with psychological well-being'. *Mindfulness*, vol. 9, no. 1, pp. 325–331.

4 Thomas, JL (1990). 'The Grandparent Role: A double bind'. *The International Journal of Aging and Human Development*, vol. 31, no. 3, pp. 169–177.

5 Kirby, JN & Sanders, MR (2012). 'Using Consumer Input to Tailor Evidence-Based Parenting Interventions to the Needs of Grandparents'. *Journal of Child and Family Studies*, vol. 21, no. 4, pp. 626–636.

6 Nyhan, B (2021). 'Why the Backfire Effect Does Not Explain the Durability of Political Misperceptions'. *PNAS*, vol. 118, no. 5.

7 Chai, BC, van der Voort, JR, Grofelnik, K, Eliasdottir, HG, Klöss, I & Perez-Cueto, FJA (2019). 'Which Diet Has the Least Environmental Impact on Our Planet? A systematic review of vegan, vegetarian and omnivorous diets'. *Sustainability*, vol. 11, no. 15.

8 Poore, J & Nemecek, T (2018). 'Reducing Food's Environmental Impacts through Producers and Consumers'. *Science*, vol. 360, no. 6392, pp. 987–992.

9 Minson, JA & Monin, B (2012). 'Do-Gooder Derogation: Disparaging morally motivated minorities to defuse anticipated reproach'. *Social Psychological and Personality Science*, vol. 3, no. 2, pp. 200–207.

10 MacInnis, CC & Hodson, G (2017). 'It Ain't Easy Eating Greens: Evidence of bias toward vegetarians and vegans from both source and target'. *Group Processes & Intergroup Relations*, vol. 20, no. 6, pp. 721–744.

11 Ruby, MB & Heine, SJ (2011). 'Meat, Morals, and Masculinity'. *Appetite*, vol. 56, no. 2, pp. 447–450.

12 ibid.

13 Markowski, KL & Roxburgh, S (2019). '"If I Became a Vegan, My Family and Friends Would Hate Me": Anticipating vegan stigma as a barrier to plant-based diets'. *Appetite*, vol. 135, pp. 1–9.

14 Axworthy, N (2019). 'Price of Lab-Grown Meat to Plummet from $280,000 to $10 Per Patty by 2021', *VegNews*, accessed online.

15 Keltner, D (2016). *The Power Paradox: How we gain and lose influence.* Penguin Books, London.

16 Merritt, AC, Effron, DA & Monin, B (2010). 'Moral Self-Licensing: When being good frees us to be bad'. *Social and Personality Psychology Compass*, vol. 4, no. 5, pp. 344–357.

17 Effron, DA, Cameron, JS & Monin, B (2009). 'Endorsing Obama Licenses Favoring Whites'. *Journal of Experimental Social Psychology*, vol. 45, no. 3, pp. 590–593.

18 Roser, M, Ritchie, H & Dadonaite, B (2013). 'Child and Infant Mortality'. *OurWorldInData.org*, accessed online.

CHAPTER 11: COMPASSION AROUND THE WORLD

1 Levine, RV, Norenzayan, A & Philbrick, K (2001). 'Cross-Cultural Differences in Helping Strangers'. *Journal of Cross-Cultural Psychology*, vol. 32, no. 5, pp. 543–560.

2 Keller, H & Kärtner, J (2013). 'Development – The cultural solution of universal developmental tasks', in Gelfand, MJ, Chiu, C & Hong, Y (eds.), *Advances in Culture and Psychology*, vol. 3, Oxford University Press, New York.

3 Henrich, J, Heine, SJ & Norenzayan, A (2010). 'The Weirdest People in the World?'. *The Behavioral and Brain Sciences*, vol. 33, no. 2–3, pp. 61–135.

4 Charities Aid Foundation (2021). 'CAF World Giving Index 2021: A global pandemic special report', *CAFonline.org*, accessed online.

5 Gelfand, MJ, Raver, RL, Nishii, L, Leslie, LM, Lun, J, Lim, BC & Van de Vliert, E (2011). 'Differences between Tight and Loose Cultures: A 33-nation study'. *Science*, vol. 332, no. 6033, pp. 1100–1104.

6 Bennett-Levy, J, Roxburgh, N, Hibner, L, Bala, S, Edwards, S, Lucre, K, Cohen, G, O'Connor, D, Keogh, S & Gilbert, P (2020). 'Arts-

Based Compassion Skills Training (ABCST): Channelling Compassion Focused Therapy through visual arts for Australia's Indigenous peoples'. *Frontiers in Psychology*, vol. 11.

7 Wilks, M, Caviola, L, Kahane, G & Bloom, P (2021). 'Children Prioritize Humans Over Animals Less than Adults Do.' *Psychological Science*, vol. 32, no. 1, pp. 27–38.

8 Köster, M, Schuhmacher, N & Kärtner, J (2015). 'A Cultural Perspective on Prosocial Development'. *Human Ethology Bulletin*, vol. 30, pp. 71–82.

9 Eisenberg, N, Fabes, RA & Spinrad, TL (2006). 'Prosocial Development', in Eisenberg, N, Damon, W & Lerner, RM (eds.), *Handbook of Child Psychology, Vol. 3: Social, emotional, and personality development*, 6th ed., John Wiley & Sons, Hoboken, pp. 646–718.

10 Schäfer, M, Haun, DBM & Tomasello, M (2015). 'Fair Is Not Fair Everywhere'. *Psychological Science*, vol. 26, no. 8, pp. 1252–1260.

11 Chernyak, N, Harvey, T, Tarullo, AR, Rockers, PC & Blake, PR (2018). 'Varieties of Young Children's Prosocial Behavior in Zambia: The role of cognitive ability, wealth, and inequality beliefs'. *Frontiers in Psychology*, vol. 9.

12 Adrian, JE, Clemente, RA, Villanueva, L & Rieffe, C (2005). 'Parent-Child Picture-Book Reading, Mothers' Mental State Language and Children's Theory of Mind'. *Journal of Child Language*, vol. 32, no. 3, pp. 673–686.

13 Kidd, DC & Castano, E (2013). 'Reading Literary Fiction Improves Theory of Mind'. *Science*, vol. 342, no. 6156, pp. 377–380.

CHAPTER 12: THE FUTURE OF COMPASSION

1 Lucas, GM, Gratch, J, King, A & Morency, L-P (2014). 'It's Only a Computer: Virtual humans increase willingness to disclose'. *Computers in Human Behavior*, vol. 37, pp. 94–100.

2 Jetten, J, Haslam, C & Haslam, SA (eds.) (2012). *The Social Cure: Identity, health and well-being*, Psychology Press, Hove.

3 Dingle, GA, Sharman, LS, Bauer, Z, Beckman, E, Broughton, M, Bunzli, E, Davidson, R, Draper, G, Fairley, S, Farrell, C, Flynn, LM, Gomersall, S, Hong, M, Larwood, J, Lee, C, Lee, J, Nitschinsk, L, Peluso, N, Reedman, SE, Vidas, D, Walter, ZC & Wright, ORL (2021). 'How Do Music Activities Affect Health and Well-Being? A scoping review of studies examining psychosocial mechanisms'. *Frontiers in Psychology*, vol. 12.

4   Marshall, JM, Dunstan, DA & Bartik, W (2020). 'Effectiveness of Using Mental Health Mobile Apps as Digital Antidepressants for Reducing Anxiety and Depression: Protocol for a multiple baseline across-individuals design'. *JMIR Research Protocols*, vol. 9, no. 7.

5   Vallor, S (2016). *Technology and the Virtues: A philosophical guide to a future worth wanting*, Oxford University Press, New York; Vallor, S (2011). 'Carebots and Caregivers: Sustaining the ethical ideal of care in the 21st century'. *Philosophy & Technology*, vol. 24, no. 3, pp. 251–268.

6   Tambe, P, Cappelli, P & Yakubovich, V (2019). 'Artificial Intelligence in Human Resources Management: Challenges and a path forward'. *California Management Review*, vol. 61, no. 4, pp. 15–42.

7   Niki, K, Okamoto, Y, Maeda, I, Mori, I, Ishii, R, Matsuda, Y, Takagi, T & Uejima, E (2019). 'A Novel Palliative Care Approach Using Virtual Reality for Improving Various Symptoms of Terminal Cancer Patients: A preliminary prospective, multicentre study'. *Journal of Palliative Medicine*, vol. 22, no. 6, pp. 702–707.

8   Brodaty, H & Donkin, M (2009). 'Family Caregivers of People with Dementia'. *Dialogues in Clinical Neuroscience*, vol. 11, no. 2, pp. 217–228.

9   World Health Organization (2021). 'Dementia'. *WHO.int*, accessed online.

EPILOGUE

1   Gilbert, P, Basran, J, MacArthur, M & Kirby, JN. 'Differences in the Semantics of Prosocial Words'.

2   Weisz, E, Ong, DC, Carlson, RW & Zaki, J (2021). 'Building Empathy Through Motivation-Based Interventions'. *Emotion*, vol. 21, no. 5, pp. 990–999.